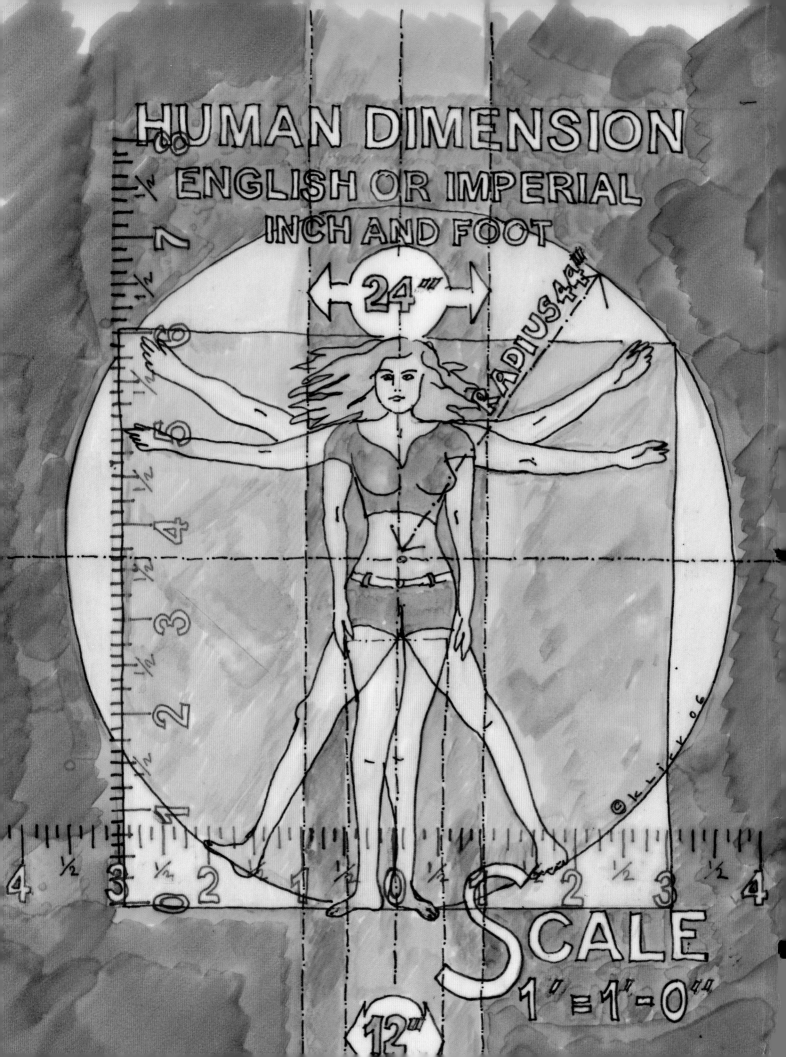

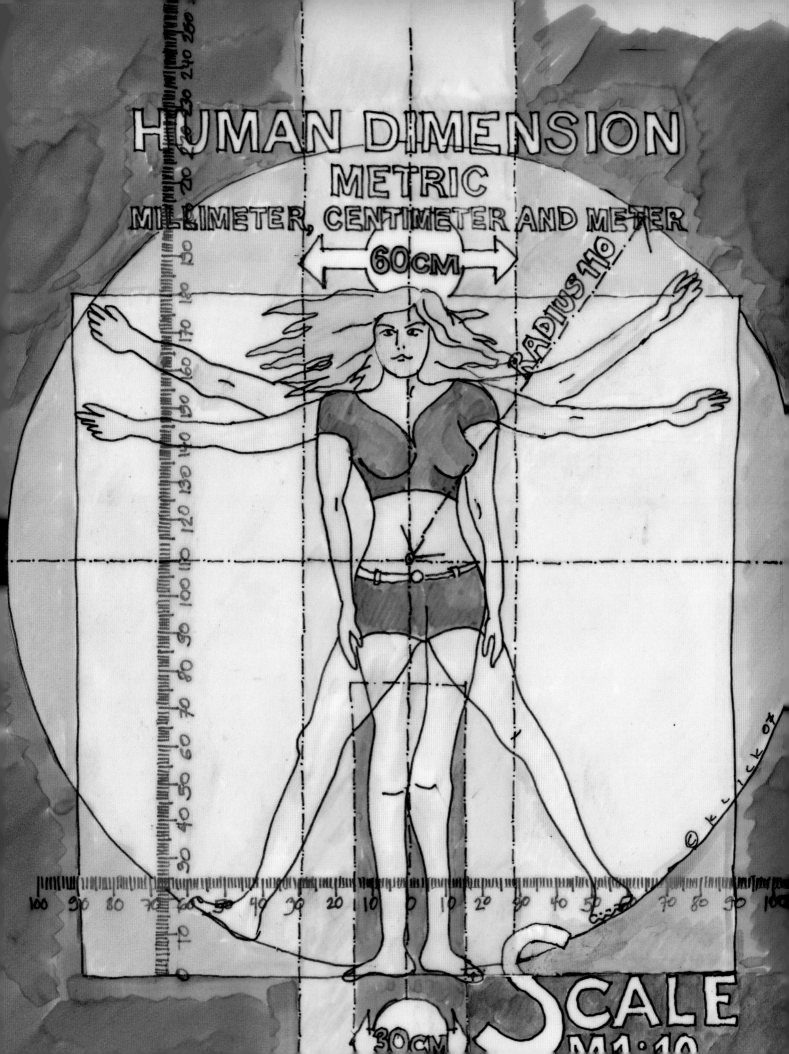

The
Interior
Designer's
LAUNCH PAD

The
Interior
Designer's
LAUNCH PAD

PETER KLICK
Harrington College of Design

FAIRCHILD BOOKS, INC.
NEW YORK

Director of Sales and Acquisitions: Dana Meltzer-Berkowitz

Executive Editor: Olga T. Kontzias

Senior Development Editor: Jennifer Crane

Art Director: Adam B. Bohannon

Production Manager: Ginger Hillman

Senior Production Editor: Elizabeth Marotta

Copyeditor: Joanne Slike

Cover and text art: Peter Klick

Library of Congress Catalog Card Number: 2007938360

ISBN: 978-1-56367-504-1

GST R 133004424

Printed in China

TP11

To all those raising
the quality of interior design
to a higher level

&

to the doctors
at Northwestern Memorial Hospital,
who saved my life.

CONTENTS

FOREWORD

This book, simply put, *is* "our" Peter: The slender, quiescent Swiss native who today teaches interior design in Chicago. He becomes talkative only in environments where he feels comfortable and where the discussion revolves around his favorite topic: interior design. Once passion, great enthusiasm, and assurance emanate from him, the spark is transferred, and it is invigorating. This is certainly what makes him a great instructor. Peter has always gone his own way with his passion. He has always silently observed the designs, layouts, and opinions of other instructors, and later even clients, but ultimately always did what he felt was right. But this book (big kudos) does not revolve around the opinions of what some egomaniac author feels is right. Instead, this starter kit, covering the basics of interior design, is intended to set the foundations for universal applications of interior design. Peter uses the human dimension and age-old experiences of craftsmen as his base. Dimensions determine form and proportion but simultaneously establish practical function. Alas, design involves functionality and, therefore, is not as pure as the arts.

This book is as unique as a fingerprint. No one has ever written—pardon me, *drawn*—about interior design like this. Peter's primary medium is not words. He has always drawn whatever occupies his mind. That is how his friends Inge and Albert Seipp have know him since their education at the Academy of the Arts in Stuttgart: "This is his way of interpreting and understanding the world." A fan of comics, like Peter, will never produce a colorless architectural sketch.

His drafts bristle with a certain human factor and they teem with vivid colors. This too is one of his strengths. His creations are molded around people. His comic-like drawings reach everyone directly through emotion. At the same time, he is providing other designers with more than just the courage to use color. He gives solid advice too. Contagion is guaranteed.

The native of Basel has always been downright handy—perhaps because he first learned the handcraft of fine woodworking and gained years of valuable work experience before commencing his postgraduate studies. Today, he is still quite the handyman, even outside the realm of his drawings. He takes apart antique furniture only to reassemble it anew. He chops the firewood for his stove, he immortalizes personal memorabilia in epoxy resin, and lately he has been responsible for creating profound collages. Everything he does is uniquely and unmistakably Peter. It is The Klick Way.

As final and personal advice from "good old Europe" given by an old companion and colleague who resorts to writing about design and who had the privilege of compiling this foreword:

Do It "The Klick Way!"
Only someone who really knows his trade can run wild and come out ahead without jeopardizing quality.

Thank you, Peter. We miss you and remain envious of such a wonderful instructor as yourself.

—ULLA ROGALSKI

BERLIN
*Design Journalist and Author,
with an education in Interior Design*

PREFACE

Who: *To anyone anywhere making decisions in interior design today.*

The result of successful interior design is harmony and positive tension. For anyone interested in interior design, the *Interior Designer's Launch Pad* teaches you in an easy way how to do successful interior design. From students to professionals, from homemakers to corporations, ask yourself, "Do I want to seriously and successfully change a space where I live or work for myself, or for someone else?" If the answer is yes, you will need this guide to succeed at interior design.

What: *Interior Designer's Launch Pad* is the new and very simple and fun tool for learning successful interior design in an easy-to-understand way for *anyone*.

When: Start now; the market needs you. Just try it. But be an educated survivor and have fun.

Why: After working in interior design production in Europe and North America for more than 30 years, I found that I could pass on my knowledge and experience about design and how to survive today in the industry and be successful through teaching. I found, however, very little material available that teaches in a simple way what rules and steps to follow. Where does anyone start to become successful in interior design?

I wanted to answer that question. I also wanted to express that interior design is *fun*. Anyone can do it, if he or she understands and learns it in an easy, uncomplicated style.

Everywhere I looked I found people with few or no skills doing poor interior design. Decorators, staff, employees, nonprofessional committees, and even mediocre architects are tasked with *designing* interiors: rooms, restaurants, offices, homes, buildings, malls, theaters, churches, and colleges. These interiors are made in indescribable ugliness, without style, without concept, without knowledge, without experience. I was very disappointed. I also found that there is a lot of misunderstanding about interior design out there. For example, interior design does not need to cost a lot of money. And good design does not have to cost more than poor design.

We, the consumers and potential interior designers, need to take responsibility and get educated. It is our style and our taste that matters and will make the difference. Design doesn't just happen. It comes from educating and understanding concept, contrast, consistency, creativity, and culture. In addition, because of the globalization of interior design, survival in the industry requires understanding the metric system. Production today is not limited to the United States but has expanded into many countries (China, Canada, Mexico, etc.) where we need to know and understand the metric system. Now, more than ever, the industry is doing business in the metric system.

I found in teaching interior design the need to define and state exactly what rules to follow. I found nothing available and decided to make a "survival guide to interior design." I started sketching my ideas using Tina, a former student of mine from Sweden who is married with two children and was designing her own home at the time. Interior design always begins with sketching. From this survival guide, the *Interior Designer's Launch Pad* was born.

ACKNOWLEDGMENTS

I would like to thank the students and faculty of Harrington College of Design for their support and assistance, without which this project would not have been possible—especially Susan Kirkman, vice president of Academics and Dean of Education; Crandon Gustafson, ID Chair; Erik Parks, President; and David Dunworth, Department Chair of Foundations and Critical Studies, for his continual motivation. Special thanks to Ryan Kapp, Program Coordinator of Foundations at Harrington, who made my European English "normal"; alumna Lisa Coduco for her critiques; and intern Sarah Schultz for her excellent renderings. I would also like to thank all my former clients and friends in Europe who trusted and believed in me, especially Bruno and Lory Franzen in Zurich, Switzerland; Albert and Inge Seipp (the best interior designers in the world) at Seipp Wohnen in Waldshut, Germany; and my teacher, Juerg Heuberger, from Laufen Ceramics in Switzerland. And last but not least, to my wife, Diane, and sons, Jimmy and Jeffrey, whom I thank for inspiring me every day. Thank you to my mother, Esther, for being my first inspiration and awakening a curiosity for interior designer in me at the age of 12. And finally, my special gratitude to Olga Kontzias at Fairchild for listening to me.

INTRODUCTION
Do You Know What Interior Design Is?

THIRTY THINGS you need to know
to become a great interior designer.

1. Interior design encompasses what you see when you close your eyes.
Imagine! Try to do it, it's amazing.

2. Interior design is visions, dreams, feelings, and emotions.
Do you have these? Yes, everyone does.

3. Interior design is opening your eyes to the world you are living in.
You have to do this to find out what you like and dislike. Discover yourself!

4. Interior design is passion and loving what you do.
Motivate yourself. If you don't love what you are doing, stop doing it and start over.

5. Interior design is taste and culture.
You can learn about good taste, and you can learn about culture too. Educate yourself. Culture is all around you. Find it and consume it.

6. Interior design is time: the past, present, and future.
The past is over and the present is almost past. Try the new: the future is exciting! If you really have to be traditional, do the research in the past and not the present. Search for the original and the true.

7. Interior design is concept.

Without a good concept there is no good design. Finding the right concept can sometimes be difficult. Try to tell a story. You also need a color concept, a light concept, and a material concept. They are fundamentals to your design concept. Try telling a story, such as the following: One day a man announced this concept: "Less is more. *Beinahe nichts* = almost nothing." This idea later made him a rich and famous architect.

8. Interior design is breaking rules.

Don't be a bore. Breaking rules is fun. Try it out; you can learn a lot. Start by doing things you never have done before. Then do things no one has ever done. (Be aware of the building codes and the lawyers.)

9. Interior design is making decisions and managing time.

You have to make decisions at the right moment. Start early and always try to stay ahead of schedule. Construct a time frame and meet the deadlines. Work ahead, and think and act for others. Take responsibility and learn from mistakes.

10. Interior design is three-dimensional.

A room consists of floors, walls, and ceilings. Learn how to think three-dimensionally. Train your spatial sense. The more you do it, the easier it gets. Be aware: floors and ceilings are horizontal surfaces; walls are vertical surfaces. Try adding color and light to your spatial sense.

11. Interior design is light and shadow. Daytime and nighttime. Daylight and artificial light. Brightness and darkness.

Light is the fourth dimension in interior design. With a good lighting concept, you can save a bad project; with a bad lighting concept, you can destroy a good project. Include your color concept in your light concept.

12. Interior design is searching for something new.

You always need to search for something new: materials, lamps, furniture, color combinations, appliances, and technical details. Educate yourself: check websites, read design, lifestyle, and architectural magazines. Stay informed of international trends. Check out the signals fashion is sending. Always know what is "in" and what is "out." What will be "in" tomorrow? Extend your antennas!

13. Interior design is mood.

The mood can be part of your concept. Yes, you can create moods with interior design. Bring the moods into your concepts.

14. Interior design is your client.

Knowing your client is essential for your success, and, sometimes, working with the client can be the most difficult part of the entire process. Research your client's personality and environment. What does he or she wear? What are his or her interests? Find out what your client likes and dislikes. Where is he or she living and working? Does he or she have a family? Learn about his or her partner, lifestyle, and culture. However, be aware that everyone thinks he or she is an interior designer. Educate your client; you are the expert! A great client will have confidence in you!

15. Interior design is function, ergonomics, and size.

What about space planning, programming, and customer needs? For what or whom are you designing? Commercial or residential? Are you designing for rehabilitation, entertainment, healthcare, or work? You have to search for the best solutions for your given set of conditions. Consider variations in the sizes of the human body in the need for adequate space for maneuverability. Yes, size matters.

16. Interior design is form.

Form follows function or function follows form. The first one is better, but you can do either. It all depends on your concept. What is your concept? For example, does it include curved walls, organic materials, angular shapes?

17. Interior design is consistency.
Be consistent with your concept and stick with it! Don't get discouraged. You have to be convinced that your project is the best solution. Believe in yourself; you are the expert.

18. Interior design is color, hue, relevance, brilliance, contrast, and temperature.
Colors are part of our lives—use them! Be aware that you are using colors in three dimensions on floors, walls, and ceilings. Colors always have relevance.

19. Interior design is "doing it."
Yes, you have to do it! Nothing gets done without the doing. It's action time!

20. Interior design is doing a great job, but always trying harder next time.
When one job is done, the next will follow. Never rest on your laurels. Review and criticize yourself with all honesty. Open your ears and listen carefully to criticism, even the least important criticism. Ask yourself: "What do I have to do better next time?" You have to improve yourself with each project. The new work never ends. Go on!

21. Interior design is material, texture, pattern, surface, and finish—hard and soft, matte, semi-gloss, and glossy.
Search for materials: there is a lot out there. Collect the ones you like for future projects, and the time will come when you are ready to use them. Be nice to reps and listen to what they have to say; you can learn a lot. Think about maintenance and security when you choose materials. For instance, harsh materials are harder to clean but less slip-

pery. Glossy materials are easier to clean but more slippery. Texture and surfaces should connect to your color concept.

22. Interior design is sound.
Don't forget the acoustics! Soft materials absorb sound; hard materials reflect sound.

23. Interior design is connecting, combining, and composing.
You have to bring all of the parts together to get the whole picture. It is like a puzzle.

24. Interior design is loving the details.
You must pay attention to all the details. If you don't know the solution, you should ask the experts.

25. Interior design is technical: electricity and appliances must be considered, as well as heating and cooling of air and water.
Learn about these from the experts; it is important. Check out foreign products. Choose wisely. Be aware, appliances have surfaces and they are part of your material and color concepts.

26. Interior design is sustainable and environmental.
Educate yourself. As designers, we have to be environmentally conscious. Redesign and restore! Search for the basics. Come to equitable decisions.

27. Interior design is arrangement.
Arrangement and placement is the final part of your project. Do it yourself. This is the best part. You can feel your design and discover the mistakes you made.

28. Interior design is about money.
Good design doesn't cost more than bad design. It is true; convince your clients of this. A good design can be done on a very low budget.

29. **Interior design is identity, whether personal or corporate.**

Personal identity is important. Do you have a business card yet? Never stop working on your portfolio. Always keep it up-to-date with your best work. Corporate identity needs a consistent corporate design from business cards to signage to logos to interior design. It is a management instrument.

30. **Interior design is making mistakes.**

Make new mistakes. Take risks. Be honest with yourself. Learn to see your mistakes. Mistakes are powerful. Mistakes can change things.

The
Interior
Designer's
LAUNCH PAD

TOOLS

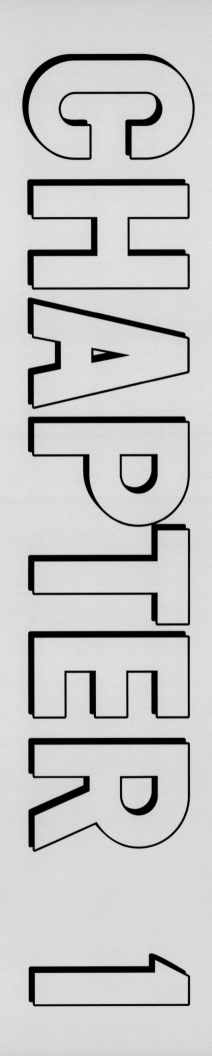

CHAPTER 1

TOOLS

THIS IS MICHAEL, TINA'S HUSBAND. HE IS AN ATTORNEY AND HE SUPPORTS TINA'S DESIGN ENDEAVORS.

THIS IS TINA: SHE WANTS TO BECOME A GREAT INTERIOR DESIGNER.

THE ADJUSTABLE LAMP BRINGS THE LIGHT WHERE YOU NEED IT.

CHAIR: ADJUSTABLE IN HEIGHT.

USE WHITE CARDBOARD UNDER YOUR DRAWING.

A DOOR SHEET AND A PAIR OF SAWHORSES ARE PERFECT AS A DRAFTING TABLE AND NOT EXPENSIVE AT ALL.

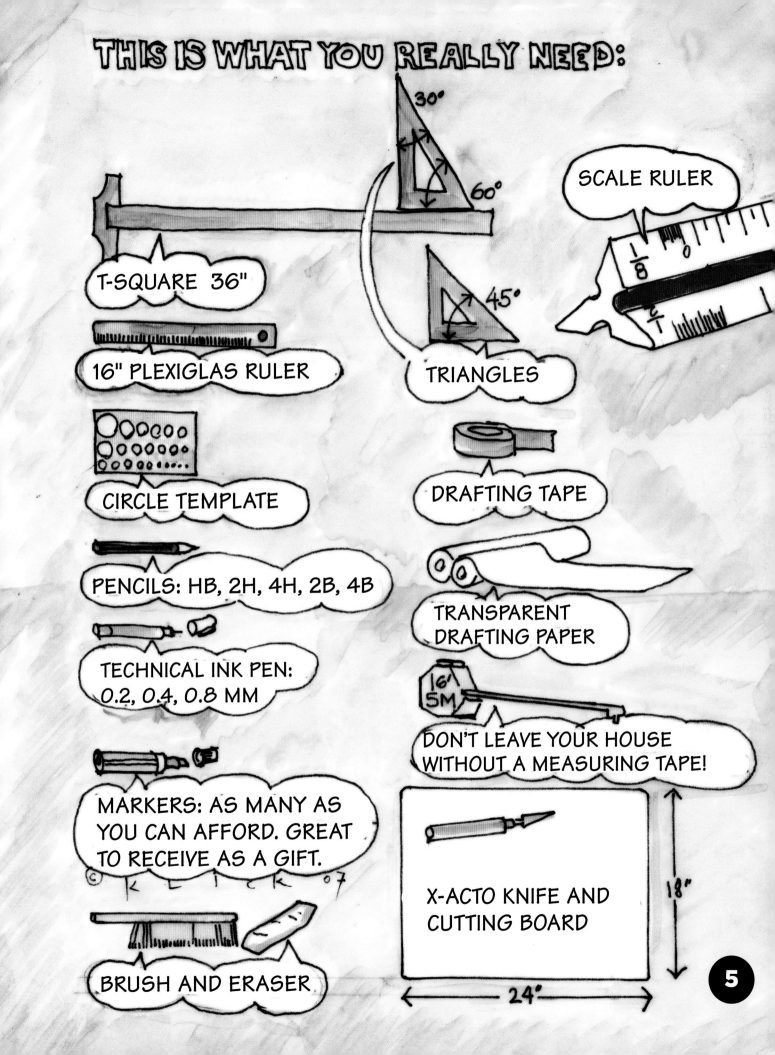

ABOUT PENCILS

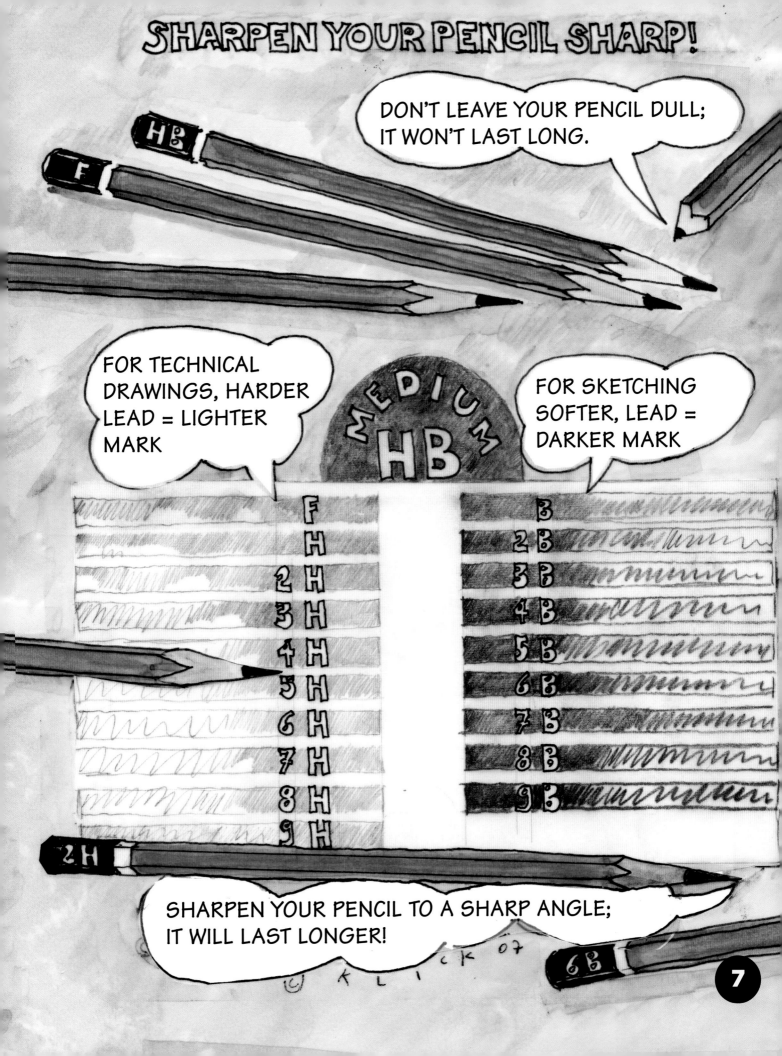

HOW TO HOLD A PENCIL

LAY THE EDGE OF YOUR HAND AND FOREARM FLAT ON THE TABLE FOR MORE STABILITY. DRAW...

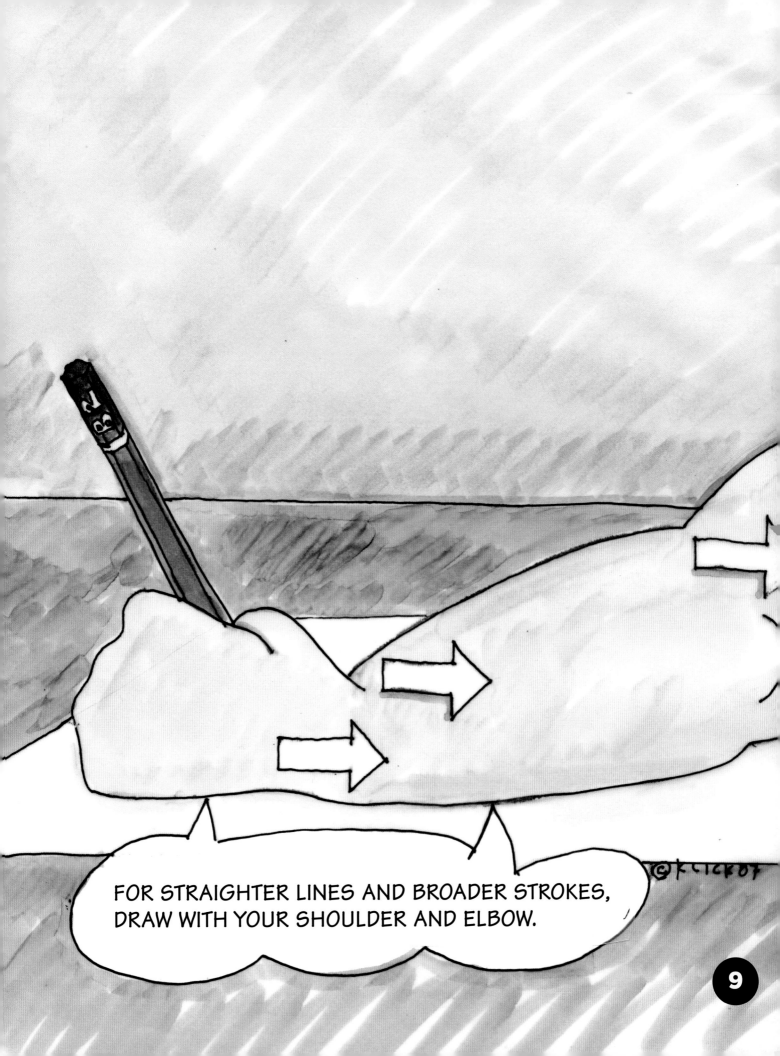

9

AVOID SHADOWS

THE LIGHT HAS TO SHINE FROM THE LEFT SIDE IF YOU ARE RIGHT-HANDED AND FROM THE RIGHT SIDE IF YOU ARE LEFT-HANDED.

FROM
CENTIMETERS
TO INCHES

CHAPTER 2

THE FROG-LEG STORY

IN A HIGH-RISE IN CHICAGO, A NEW ENTRANCE HALL WAS CONSTRUCTED. IT WAS MADE COMPLETELY OUT OF GLASS AND WAS IN THE FORM OF A CUBE. THE SIZE OF THE GLASS CUBE WAS 90-FEET WIDE, 90-FEET DEEP, AND 90-FEET HIGH. TO HOLD THE GLASS PANELS TO THE STRUCTURE, THE BUILDERS USED PRECISE STAINLESS-STEEL HARDWARE CALLED FROGLEGS. TO SAVE ON COSTS, THE 68 PARTS WERE ORDERED IN CHINA. THE MANUFACTURER MADE A MISTAKE IN CONVERTING INCHES INTO CENTIMETERS AND MILLIMETERS, AND ALL THE PARTS WERE DELIVERED IN THE WRONG DIMENSIONS. THE HARDWARE HAD TO BE REORDERED, WHICH CAUSED A DELAY FOR THE CONSTRUCTION SITE FOR ABOUT EIGHT MONTHS. THE ESTIMATED ADDITIONAL COST TO FIX THIS ERROR WAS $120,000. BE AWARE THAT WHEN YOU DEAL WITH CENTIMETERS AND INCHES, YOU MUST CONVERT THE MEASUREMENTS CORRECTLY.

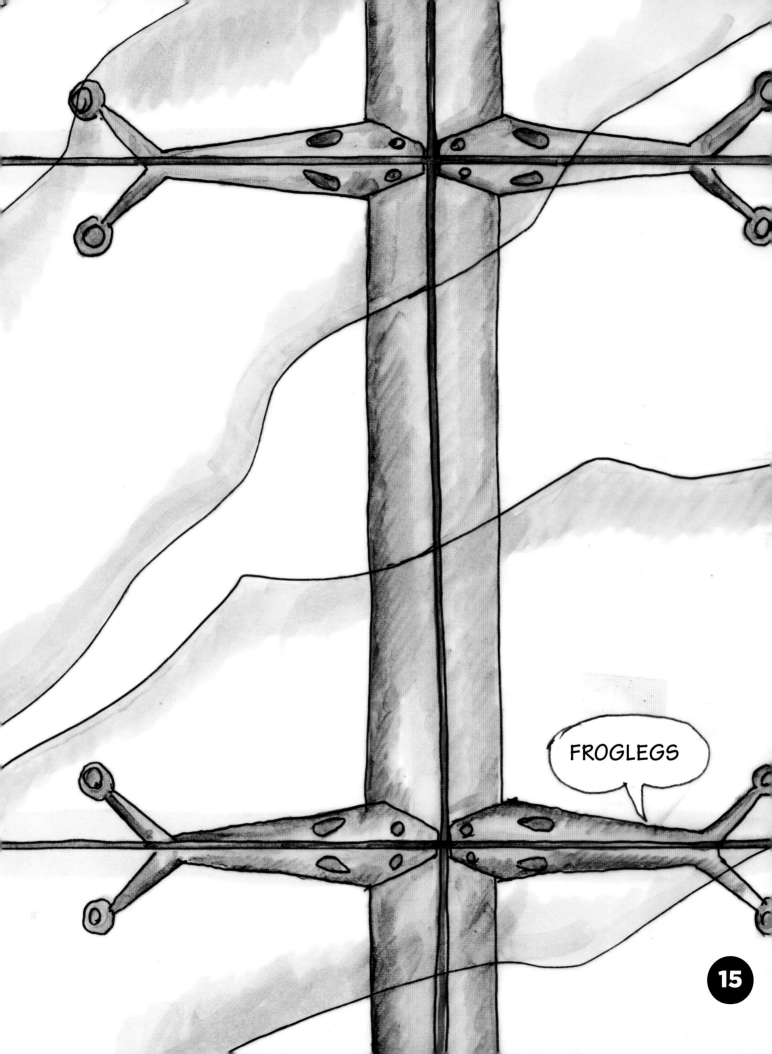

HOW TO READ INCHES AND CENTIMETERS

THE DIFFERENCE BETWEEN THE TWO MEASURING SYSTEMS IS THAT ENGLISH (INCHES) USES FRACTIONS AND METRIC (CENTIMETERS) USES THE DECIMAL SYSTEM. THE DECIMAL SYSTEM MAKES IT MUCH EASIER TO FIGURE OUT CALCULATIONS, ESPECIALLY WHEN YOU HAVE TO DIVIDE. CALCULATING STAIRS IN INCHES IS A MUCH MORE DIFFICULT TASK THAN USING CENTIMETERS. MANY STAIR BUILDERS AND KITCHEN CABINET BUILDERS IN THE UNITED STATES USE THE METRIC SYSTEM.

IF YOU COMPARE THE STANDARD SIZES IN METRIC AND ENGLISH, YOU WILL FIND THAT THEY ARE DIFFERENT. YOU CANNOT JUST CONVERT THEM. YOU HAVE TO MEMORIZE THEM.

FROM CENTIMETERS TO INCHES

COMPARE METRIC WITH ENGLISH ON THIS CHART. REMEMBER, YOU ABSOLUTELY NEED TO KNOW THE FOLLOWING: 1 YARD IS 91.4 CM, 1 FOOT IS 30.48 CM, AND 1 INCH IS 2.54 CM.

METRIC ←→ ENGLISH

MM MILLIMETER	CM CENTIMETER	M METER		YARD	FEET	INCH
1 MM	0.1 CM	0.001 M	→	0.00108... YARD	0.00328... FEET	0.03937... INCH
10 MM	**1** CM	0.01 M	→	0.01093... YARD	0.32808... FEET	0.39378... INCH
1000 MM	100 CM	**1** M	→	1.09361... YARD	3.28083... FEET	39.3700... INCH
914 MM	91.4 CM	0.9144 M	←	**1** YARD	3 FEET	36 INCH
304.8 MM	30.48 CM	0.3048 M	→	0.3333... YARD	**1** FOOT	12 INCH
25.4 MM	2.54 CM	0.0254 M	→	0.0277... YARD	0.8333... FEET	**1** INCH

©KLICK

19

FROM CENTIMETERS TO INCHES

YOU NEED PRECISE DIMENSIONS, SO USE THIS TYPE OF MEASURING TAPE.

THIS RULER SHOWS FRACTIONS AND THE DECIMAL SYSTEM. IT IS EASIER TO USE FRACTIONS FOR INCHES.

THIS IS A 400% ENLARGEMENT OF THE RULER ABOVE.

FROM CENTIMETERS TO INCHES

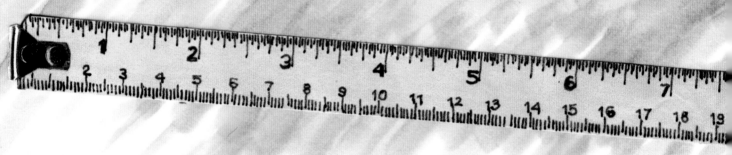

MEASURING TAPES

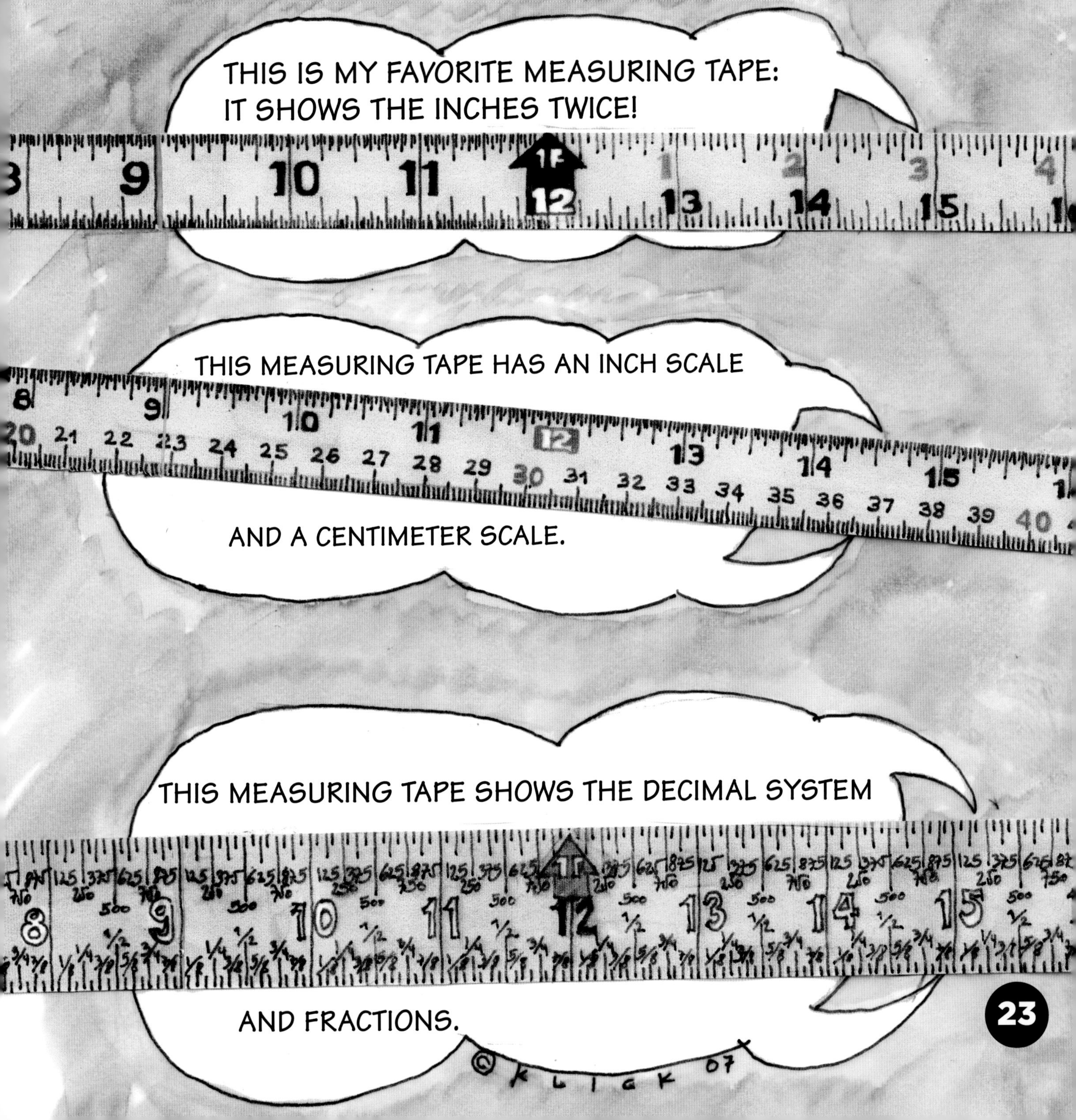

THIS IS MY FAVORITE MEASURING TAPE:
IT SHOWS THE INCHES TWICE!

THIS MEASURING TAPE HAS AN INCH SCALE

AND A CENTIMETER SCALE.

THIS MEASURING TAPE SHOWS THE DECIMAL SYSTEM

AND FRACTIONS.

© KLICK 07

23

FROM CENTIMETERS TO INCHES

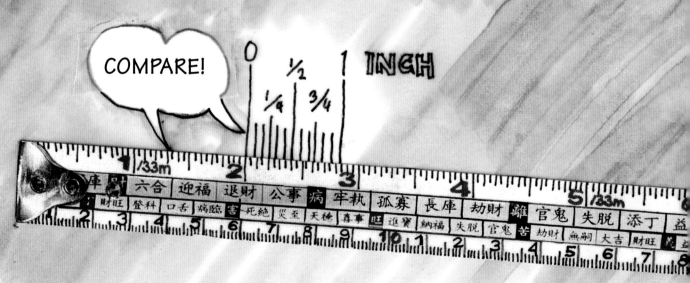

"DOUBLE METER" (TWO METERS) MY FAVORITE METRIC MEASURING TOOL MADE IN BEECH WOOD: FOLD OUT.

METRIC: METERS (M), CENTIMETERS (CM), AND MILLIMETERS (MM) 1M = 100 CM, 1CM = 10MM

BE AWARE! PING, AN OLD JAPANESE MEASURING SYSTEM THAT IS ALSO UNOFFICIALLY USED IN TAIWAN, IS ALMOST AN INCH, BUT NOT QUITE.

LINEAR vs. AREA vs. SPACE

LINEAR IS ONE-DIMENSIONAL

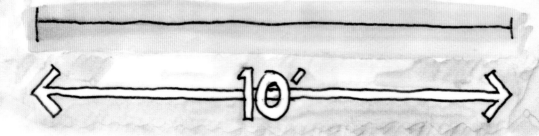

10'

10' LENGTH × 10' WIDTH = 100 SQUARE FEET

AREA IS TWO-DIMENSIONAL

100 SQUARE FEET

10' WIDTH

10' LENGTH

10' LENGTH × 10' WIDTH = 100 SQUARE FEET × 10' HEIGHT = 1,000 CUBIC FEET

SPACE IS THREE-DIMENSIONAL

1,000 CUBIC FEET

10' HEIGHT

10' WIDTH

10' LENGTH

©KLICK07

SCALE: 1/2" = 1'-0"

LINEAR vs. AREA vs. SPACE
METRIC

LINEAR

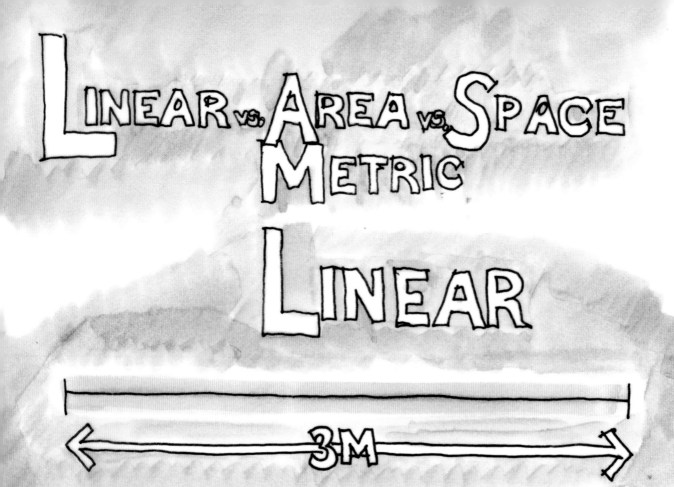

3M

3M LENGTH × 3M WIDTH = 9 SQUARE METERS (M²)

AREA

9M²

3M WIDTH

3M
LENGTH

SCALES

CHAPTER 3

HOW TO READ SCALES

THE SCALE HELPS YOU TO DRAW IN A REDUCED SIZE.

THE INTERIOR DESIGNER NEEDS THE FOLLOWING SCALES:

IN CENTIMETERS:

$1:100$ $1:50$ $1:20$ $1:10$

IN INCHES:

$\frac{1}{8}'' = 1'0''$ $\frac{1}{4}'' = 1'0''$ $\frac{1}{2}'' = 1'0''$ $1'' = 1'0''$

USE A SMALL SCALE FOR LARGE FLOOR PLANS.

USE FOR FLOOR PLANS AND ELEVATIONS.

USE FOR DETAILED FLOOR PLANS, ELEVATIONS, AND SECTIONS. FOR KITCHENS AND BATHROOMS, USE WITH DIMENSIONS.

USE FOR FURNITURE AND DETAILS. USE WITH DIMENSIONS.

©KLICK 07

HOW TO READ SCALES

THIS SCALE SHOWS 1/4 INCH AS 1 FOOT

1/4 in = 1 ft

1/8 in = 1 ft

THIS SCALE SHOWS 1/8 INCH AS 1 FOOT

1/4 in = 1 ft

THIS IS A 400% ENLARGEMENT OF THE SCALE ABOVE

1/8 in = 1 ft

THE SCALE HELPS YOU TO DRAW IN A REDUCED SIZE

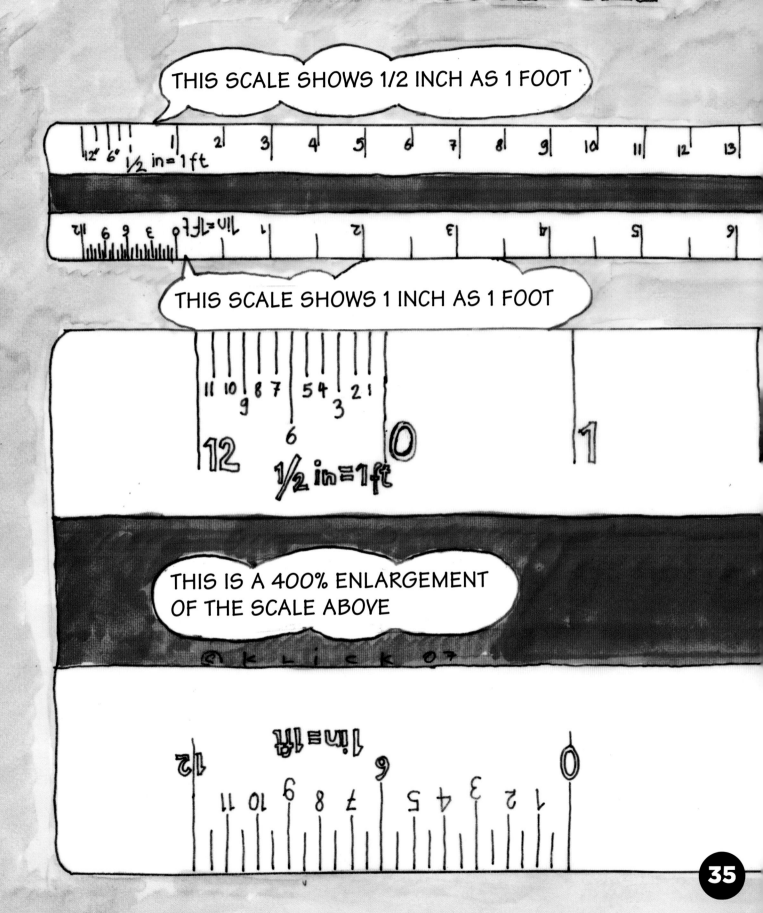

HOW TO READ SCALES

THE METRIC SYSTEM USES THE DECIMAL SYSTEM

1 METER HAS
100 CENTIMETERS

1 CENTIMETER HAS
10 MILLIMETERS

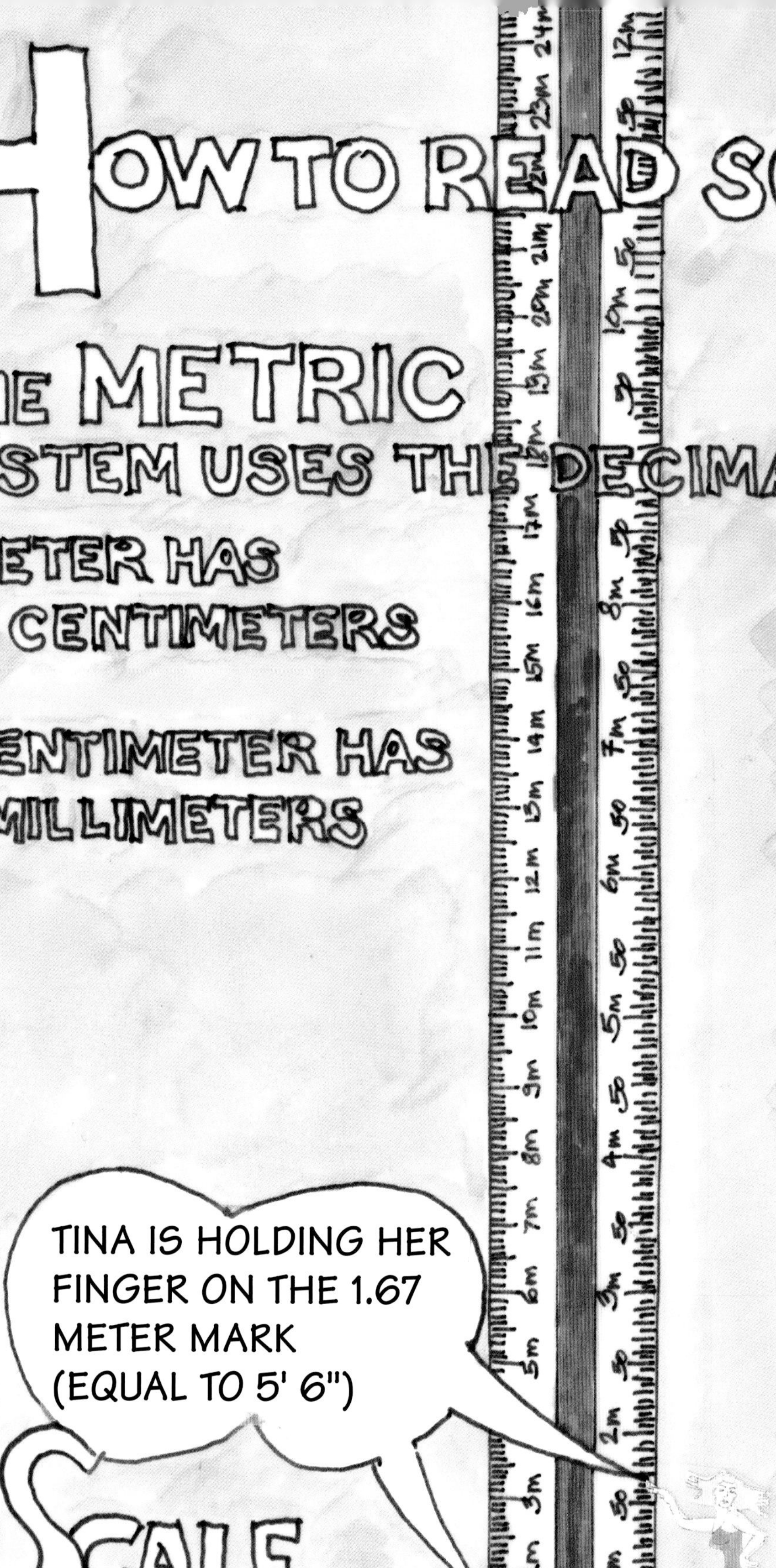

SCALE 1:100

1 METER =
5 CENTIMETERS

SCALE 1:50

1 METER =
2 CENTIMETERS

1 METER (M) IS 100 CENTIMETERS (CM)
1 CENTIMETER IS 10 MILLIMETERS (MM)

METRIC SCALES ARE EASY
MATH. YOU DON'T NEED A
CALCULATOR FOR THIS:

1:10   1M = 10 CM
DIVIDE 100 CM BY 10

1:20   1M = 5 CM
DIVIDE 10 CM BY 2 OR 100 CM BY 20

1:50   1M = 2CM
DIVIDE 10 CM BY 5 OR 100 CM BY 50

1:100 1M = 1CM
DIVIDE 10 CM BY 10 OR 100 CM BY 100

41

© KLICK

THE SCALES

THIS IS TINA'S HOUSE. IT IS SKETCHED IN DIFFERENT SCALES. COMPARE THE SCALES USED BY INTERIOR DESIGNERS.

42

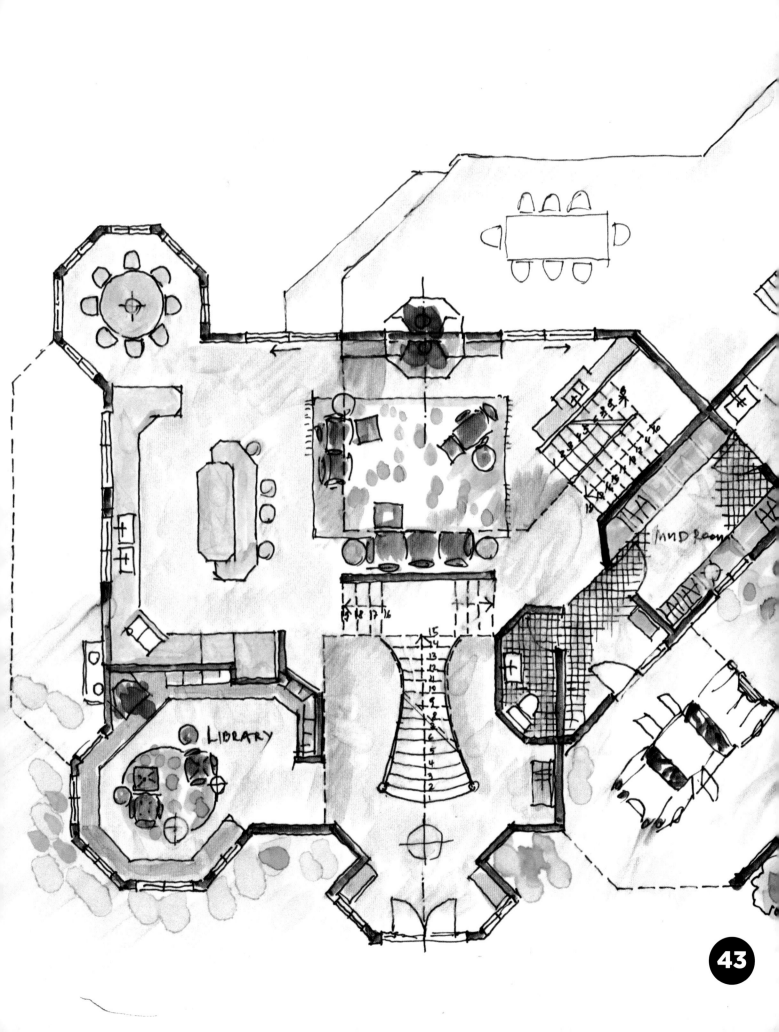

LIBRARY

MUD ROOM

43

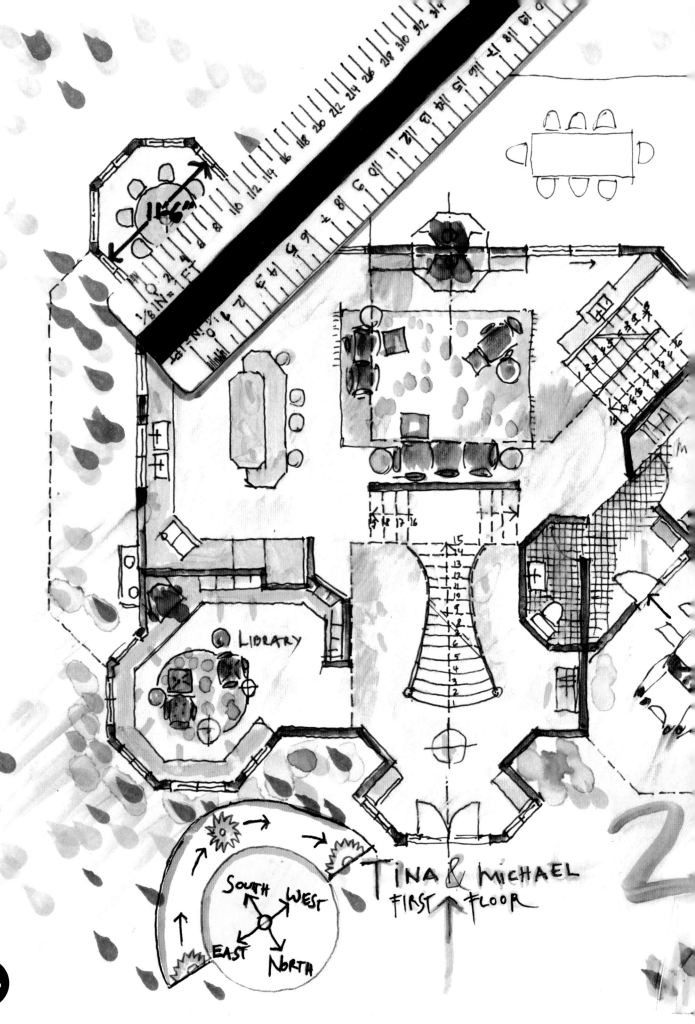

LIBRARY

TINA & MICHAEL
FIRST FLOOR

SOUTH
WEST
EAST
NORTH

SCALE

1/8 " = 1'-00"

1/8" = 1'-00" IS SIMILAR TO 1:100
THIS IS A SMALL SCALE. YOU NEED IT FOR
LARGER PROJECTS, SUCH AS A HOUSE.

©klick 07

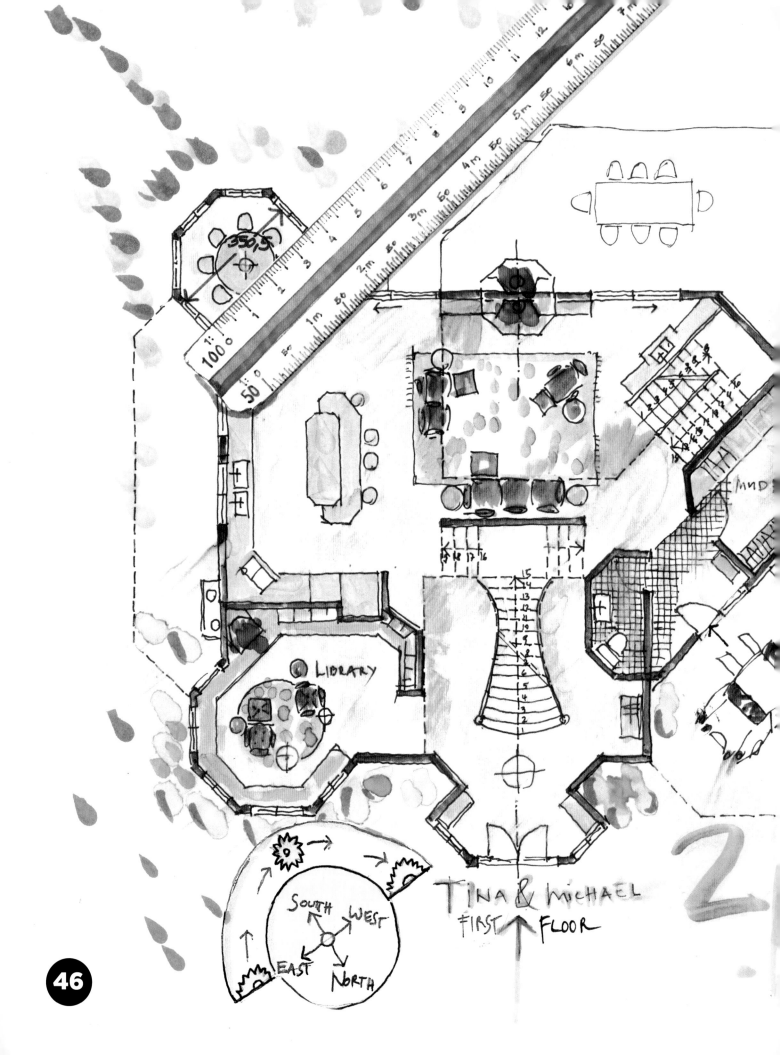

350,5

1:
100

LIBRARY

MUD

TINA & MICHAEL
FIRST FLOOR

SOUTH   WEST

EAST   NORTH

46

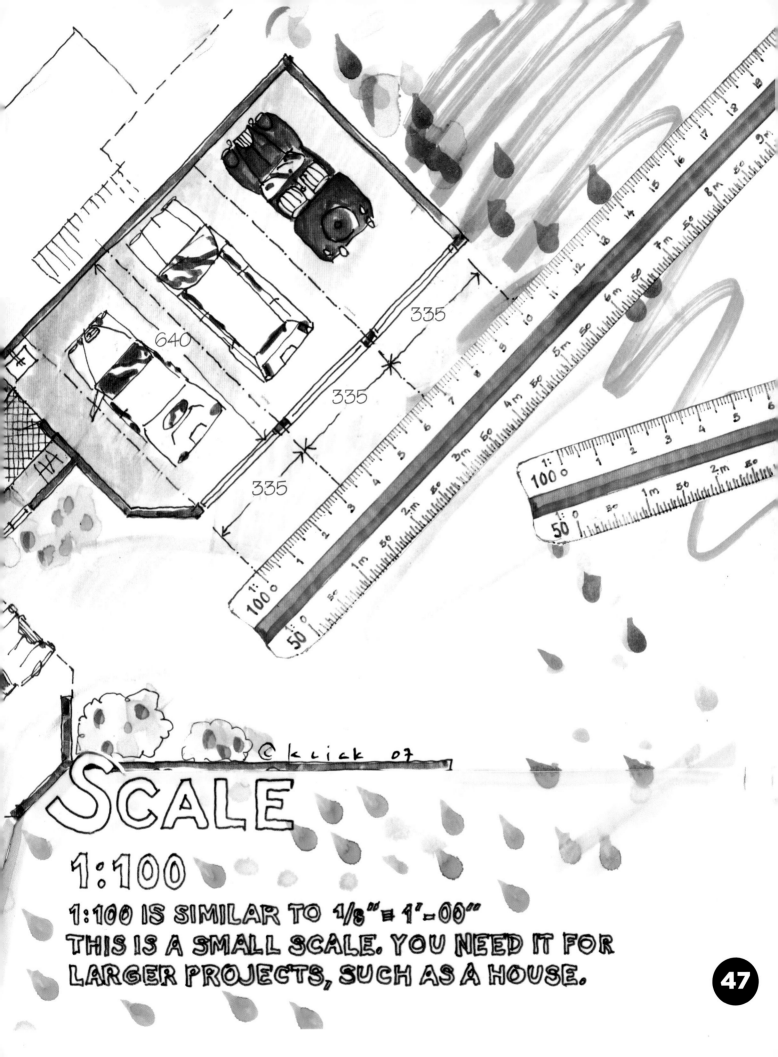

640

335

335

335

© klick 07

SCALE

1:100

1:100 IS SIMILAR TO 1/8" = 1'-00"
THIS IS A SMALL SCALE. YOU NEED IT FOR
LARGER PROJECTS, SUCH AS A HOUSE.

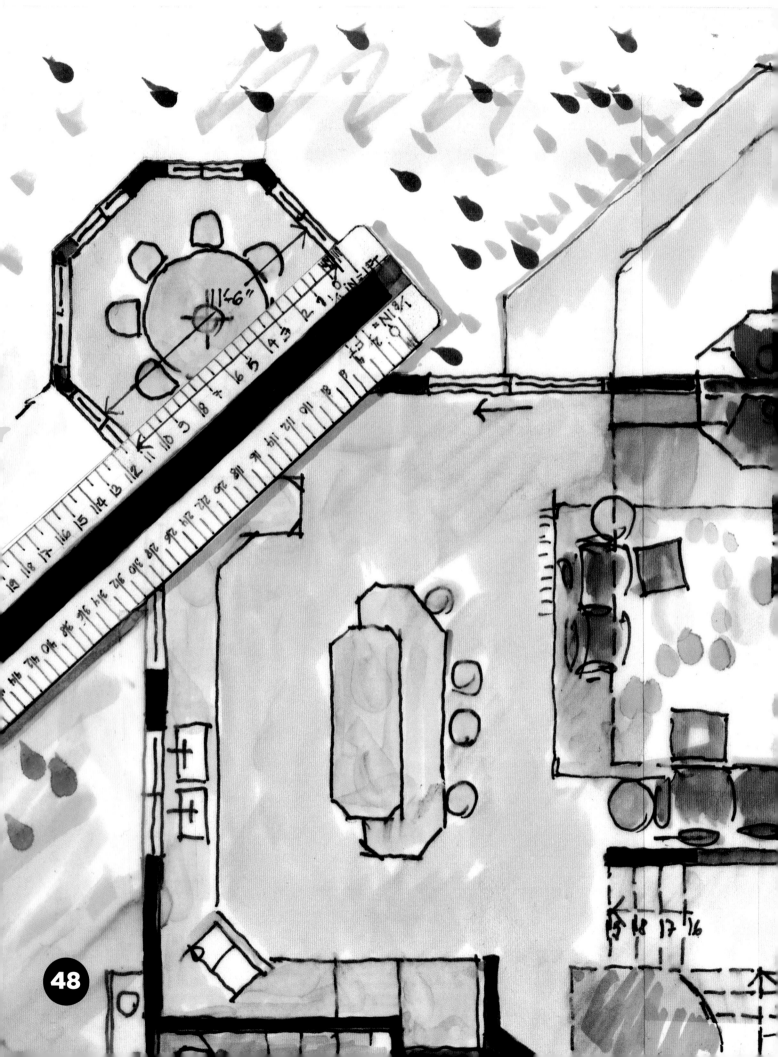

SCALE

1/4" = 1'-00"

1/4" = 1'-00" IS SIMILAR TO 1:50
THIS SCALE IS DOUBLE THE
SIZE OF 1/8" = 1'0"
USE THIS SCALE TO DRAW
ROOMS OR SMALL HOUSES.

© KLICK 07 →

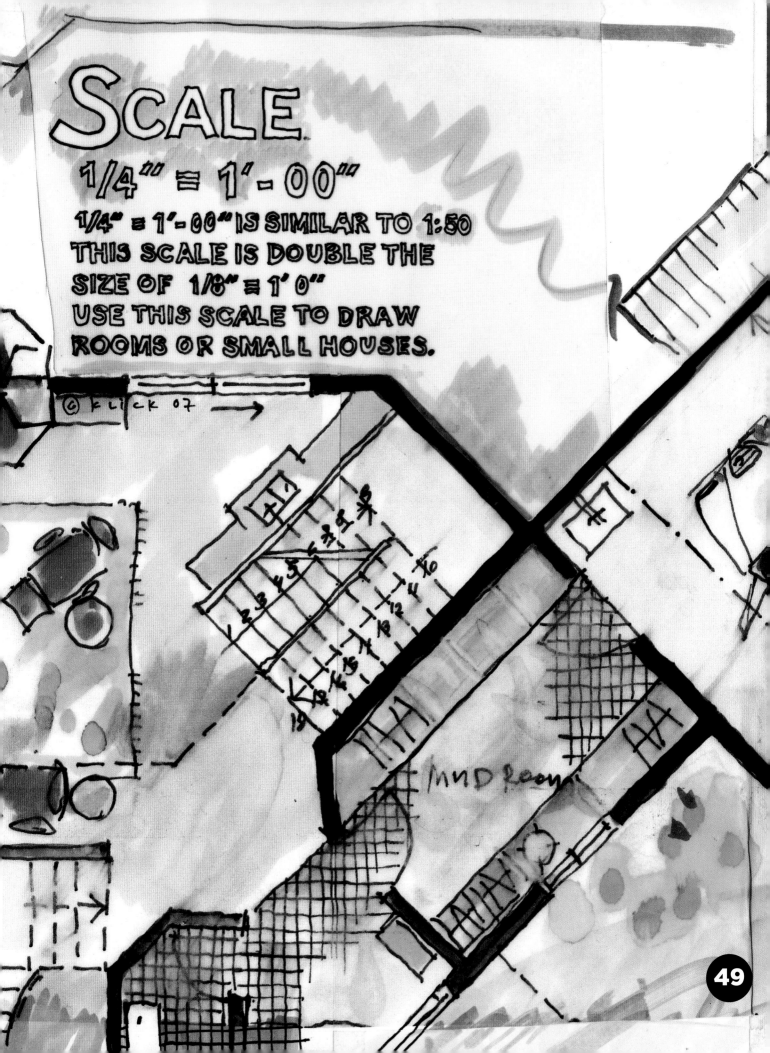

MUD ROOM

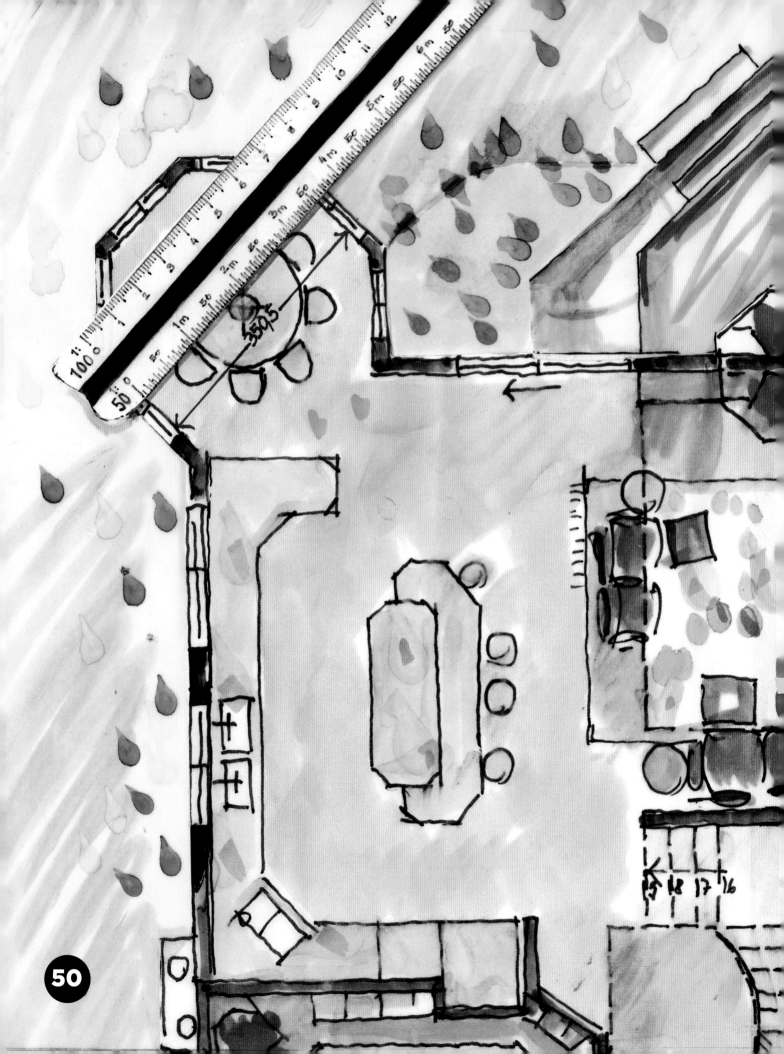

SCALE

1:50

1:50 IS SIMILAR TO 1/4"=1'-00"
THIS SCALE IS DOUBLE THE
SIZE OF 1:100
USE THIS SCALE TO DRAW
ROOMS OR SMALL HOUSES.

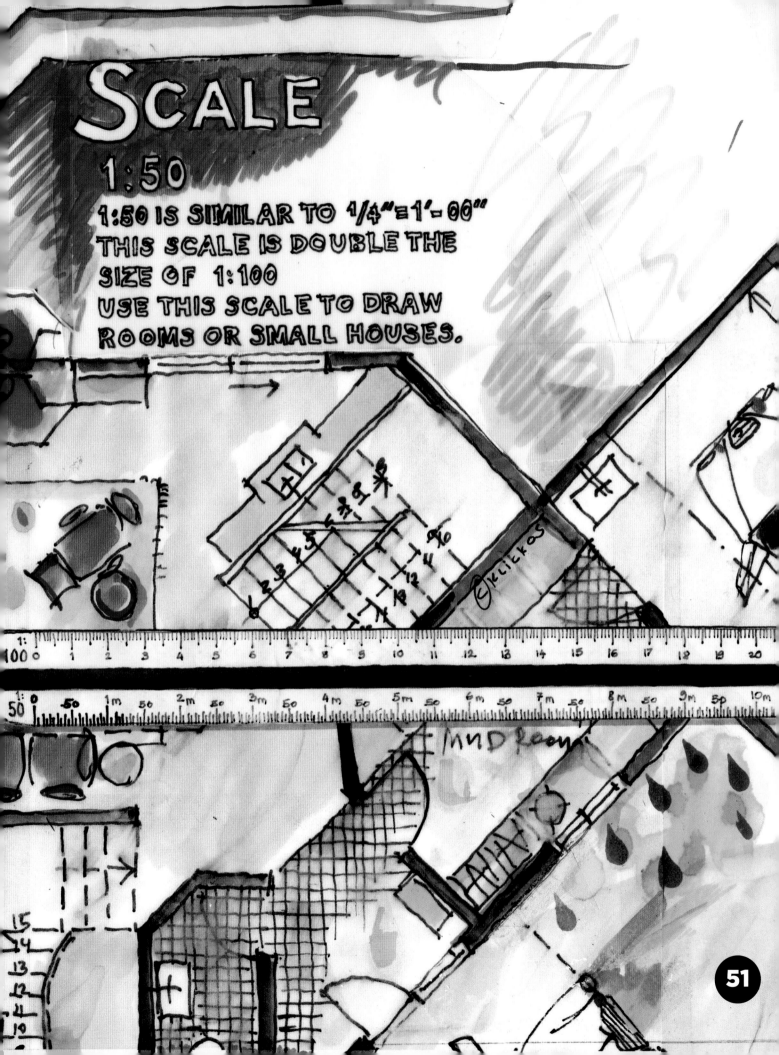

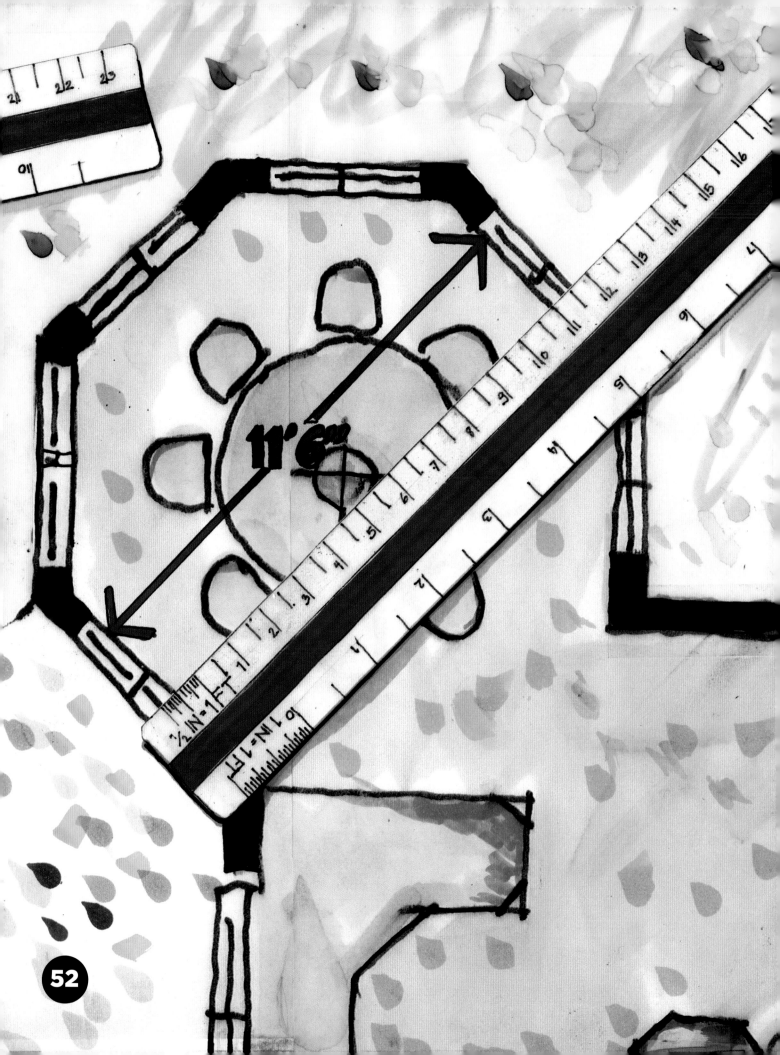

11'6"

½ IN-1FT

1 IN-1FT

52

SCALE
1/2" = 1'- 00"

1/2" = 1'- 00" IS SIMILAR TO 1:20
THIS SCALE IS DOUBLE THE
SIZE OF 1/4" = 1' 0"
YOU WILL NEED THIS SCALE TO DRAW
SMALL OR MORE DETAILED ROOMS.

½ IN=1FT   1   2   3   4   5   6   7   8   9

1 IN=1FT   0   1   2   3   4

© KLICK 07

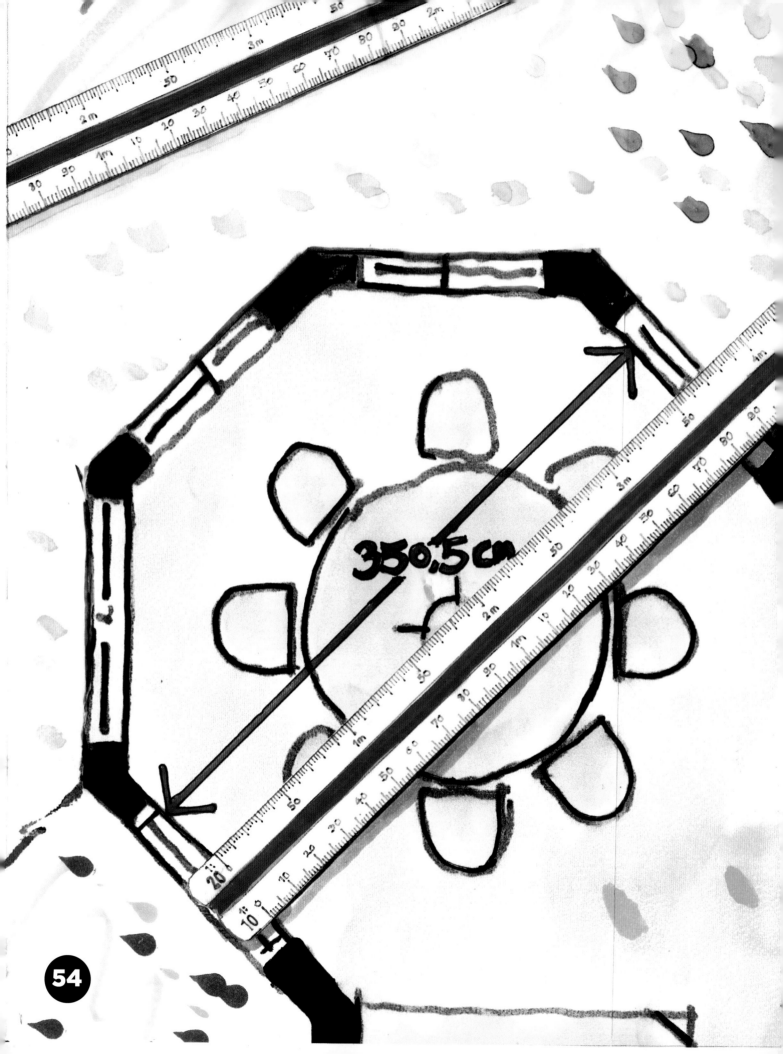

350,5 cn

SCALE

1:20

1:20 IS SIMILAR TO 1/2" = 1'-00"
YOU WILL NEED THIS SCALE TO DRAW
SMALL OR MORE DETAILED ROOMS.

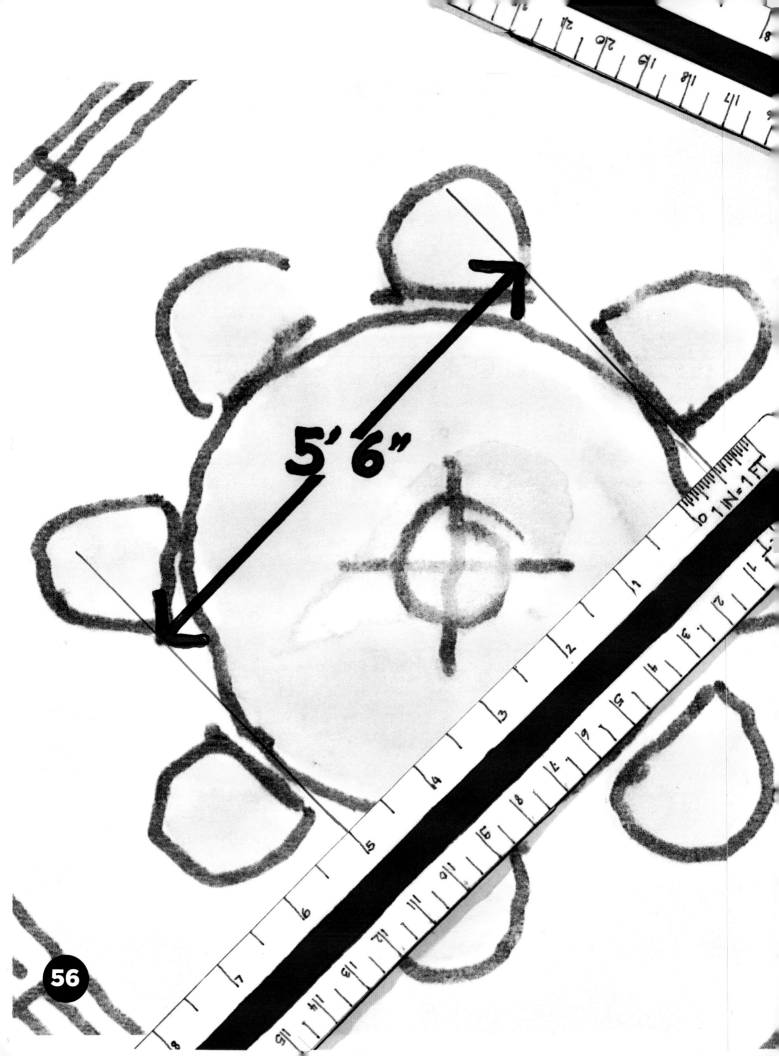

5' 6"

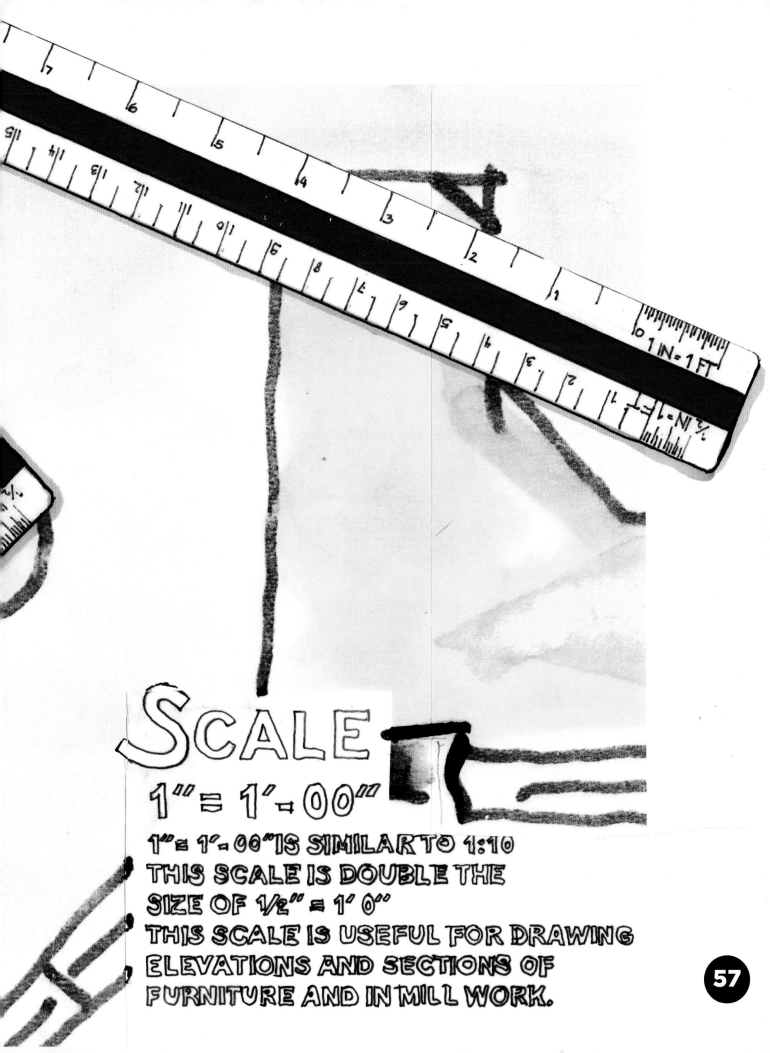

SCALE

1" = 1'-00"

1" = 1'-00" IS SIMILAR TO 1:10
THIS SCALE IS DOUBLE THE
SIZE OF 1/2" = 1' 0"
THIS SCALE IS USEFUL FOR DRAWING
ELEVATIONS AND SECTIONS OF
FURNITURE AND IN MILL WORK.

57

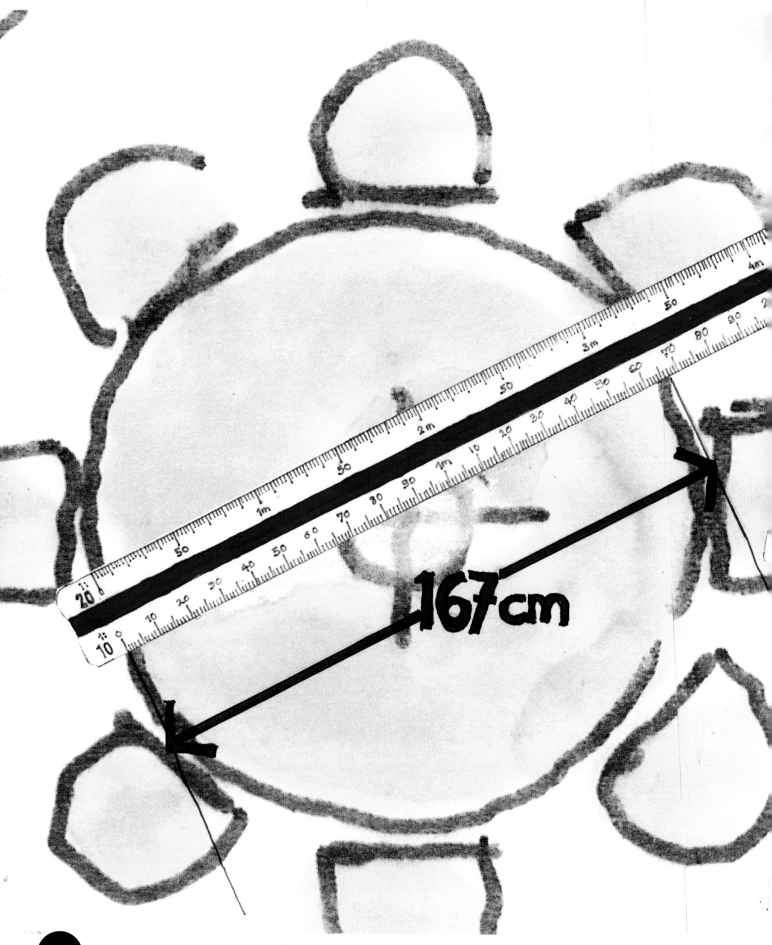

167cm

SCALE

1:10

1:10 IS SIMILAR TO 1" = 1'-00"
THIS SCALE IS DOUBLE THE
SIZE OF 1:20
THIS SCALE IS USEFUL FOR DRAWING
ELEVATIONS AND SECTIONS OF
FURNITURE AND IN MILL WORK.

CONVERT SCALES: ENLARGE AND REDUCE ON YOUR COPIER:

1" = 1'-0" TO 1:10 USE 120%

½" = 1'-0" TO 1:20 USE 120%

¼" = 1'-0" TO 1:50 USE 96%

⅛" = 1'-0" TO 1:100 USE 96%

1:10 TO 1" = 1'-0" USE 83%

1:20 TO ½" = 1'-0" USE 83%

1:50 TO ¼" = 1'-0" USE 103%

1:100 TO ⅛" = 1'-0" USE 103%

© KLICK 07

UNKNOWN SCALES

EVERY REAL ESTATE FLOOR PLAN WILL NOT BE IN SCALES. THERE WILL PROBABLY BE A DIMENSION ON THE PLAN THAT WILL HELP YOU CONVERT IT TO A USABLE SCALE.

IF THERE IS NO DIMENSION PROVIDED, REMEMBER THAT ENTRY DOORS ARE ALWAYS DRAWN 3-FEET OR 90-CENTIMETERS WIDE.

LEARN HOW TO CONVERT UNKNOWN SCALES TO CHOSEN SCALES.

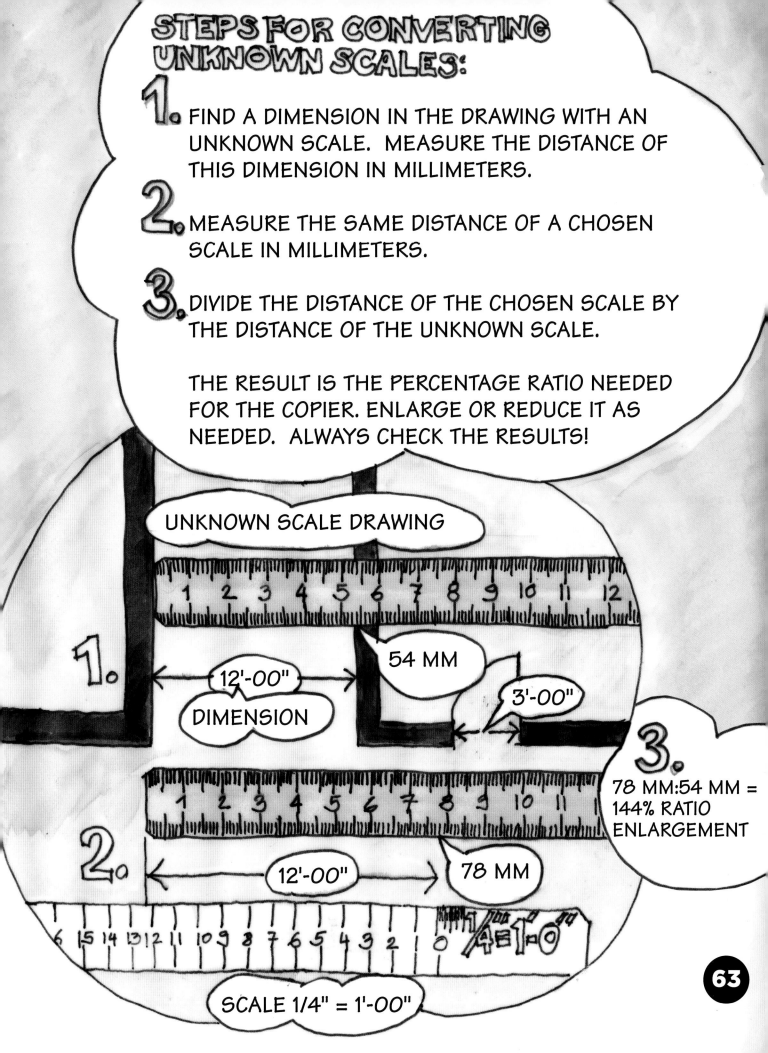

STEPS FOR CONVERTING UNKNOWN SCALES:

1. FIND A DIMENSION IN THE DRAWING WITH AN UNKNOWN SCALE. MEASURE THE DISTANCE OF THIS DIMENSION IN MILLIMETERS.

2. MEASURE THE SAME DISTANCE OF A CHOSEN SCALE IN MILLIMETERS.

3. DIVIDE THE DISTANCE OF THE CHOSEN SCALE BY THE DISTANCE OF THE UNKNOWN SCALE.

THE RESULT IS THE PERCENTAGE RATIO NEEDED FOR THE COPIER. ENLARGE OR REDUCE IT AS NEEDED. ALWAYS CHECK THE RESULTS!

UNKNOWN SCALE DRAWING

1.

12'-00"

DIMENSION

54 MM

3'-00"

3. 78 MM:54 MM = 144% RATIO ENLARGEMENT

2.

12'-00"

78 MM

SCALE 1/4" = 1'-00"

1/4"=1'-0"

HOW TO CONVERT
ENGLISH TO METRIC AND METRIC TO ENGLISH

CONVERT ENGLISH TO METRIC AND METRIC TO ENGLISH ON YOUR FAVORITE SEARCH ENGINE

Favorite Search Engine

JUST TYPE YOUR REQUEST DIRECTLY IN THE SEARCH FIELD: 5 feet in cm | Search

Search **Web** Images Groups News

`5 feet in cm` [Search]

Web

 5 feet = 152.4 centimeters

More about the calculator.

Search for documents containing the terms *5 feet in cm.*

© KLICK 07

FLOORPLANS, ELEVATIONS, AND SECTIONS

CHAPTER 4

FLOORPLANS, ELEVATIONS, AND SECTIONS

A *FLOOR PLAN* IS A PLAN VIEW FROM ABOVE, OR A *PLAN VIEW*.

AN *ELEVATION* IS A VIEW OF THE FACE OF AN OBJECT OR THE FACE OF A WALL IN A ROOM.

A *SECTION* IS A CUT THROUGH A ROOM, A BUILDING, OR FURNITURE. EVERY SECTION HAS ELEVATION LINES, OR AN ELEVATION WHERE YOU SEE WHAT IS HAPPENING "BEHIND" THE CUT.

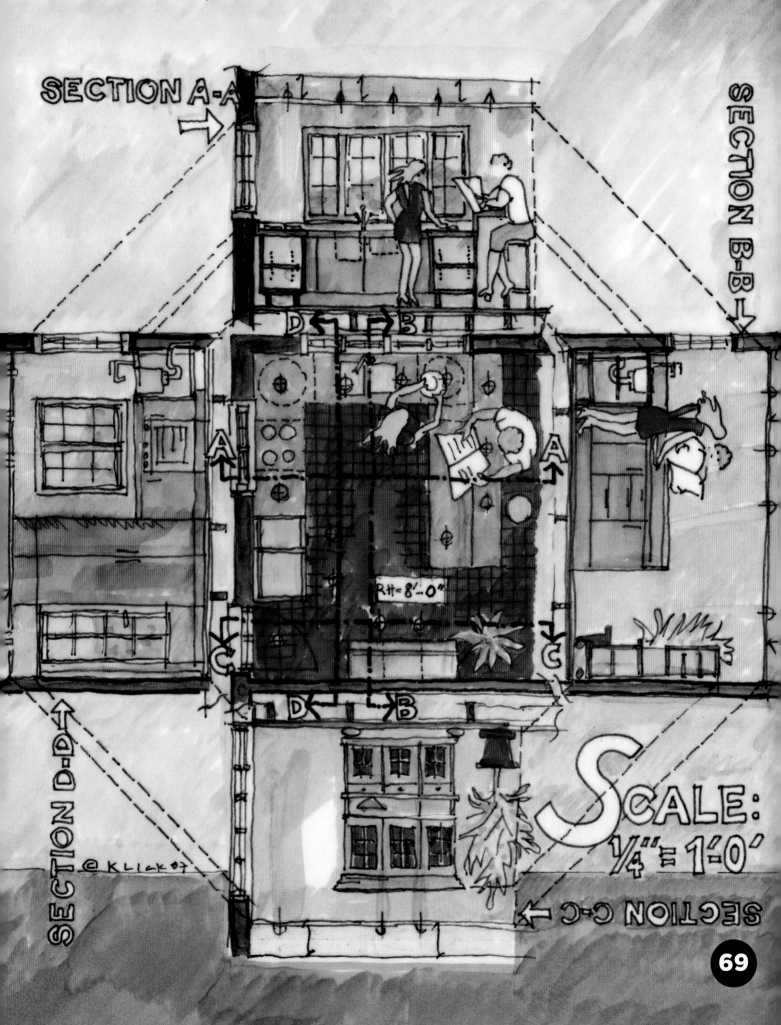

ELEVATION AND SECTION

LEFT ELEVATION

SCALE: 1" = 1'-0"

70

SECTION B-B

FRONT ELEVATION

SECTION A-A

SECTION C-C

©KLICK 07

71

SIZE
MATTERS

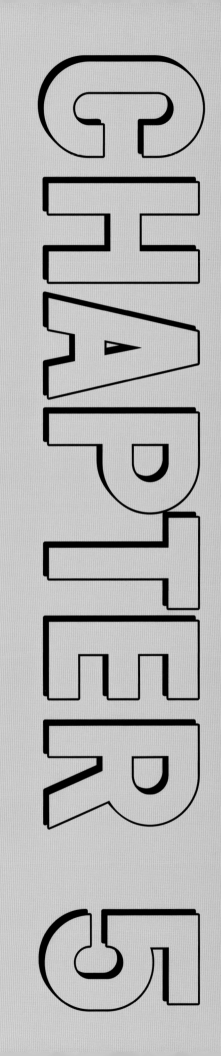

CHAPTER 5

SIZE MATTERS

THE HUMAN BODY IS THE BASIS FOR EVERYTHING IN INTERIOR DESIGN. WITH THIS IN MIND, BE CAREFUL AS MISTAKES CAN BE COSTLY.

I ONCE DESIGNED A BEAUTIFUL BATHROOM WITH A GREAT DOUBLE VANITY AND FANTASTIC BLACK-AND-SILVER SPARKLING GRANITE COUNTERTOP. THE LOOK WAS MAGNIFICENT AND THE CLIENT WAS VERY HAPPY. I WAS PLEASED, TOO.

NOT FOR LONG, HOWEVER.

AFTER THE FIRST WEEK OF USING THE VANITY, MY CLIENT COMPLAINED THAT HE COULD NOT REACH THE FAUCET TO GET WATER IN HIS MOUTH BY BENDING OVER THE COUNTERTOP BECAUSE HIS BELLY WAS IN THE WAY. HE WAS FRUSTRATED BECAUSE HE HAD BRUSHED HIS TEETH IN THIS FASHION FOR YEARS.

TO SATISFY THE CLIENT, I ENDED UP COMPLETELY REDOING THE BEAUTIFUL GRANITE COUNTERTOP BY MOVING THE SINK AND THE FAUCET 1 1/2 INCHES CLOSER TO THE FRONT.

FINAL ADDITIONAL COSTS FOR ME: $4,000.

THE MORAL OF THE STORY IS THAT SIZE MATTERS. NEVER LEAVE YOUR HOUSE WITHOUT YOUR MEASURING TAPE! ALWAYS CHECK YOUR CLIENTS' ACCESSIBILITY.

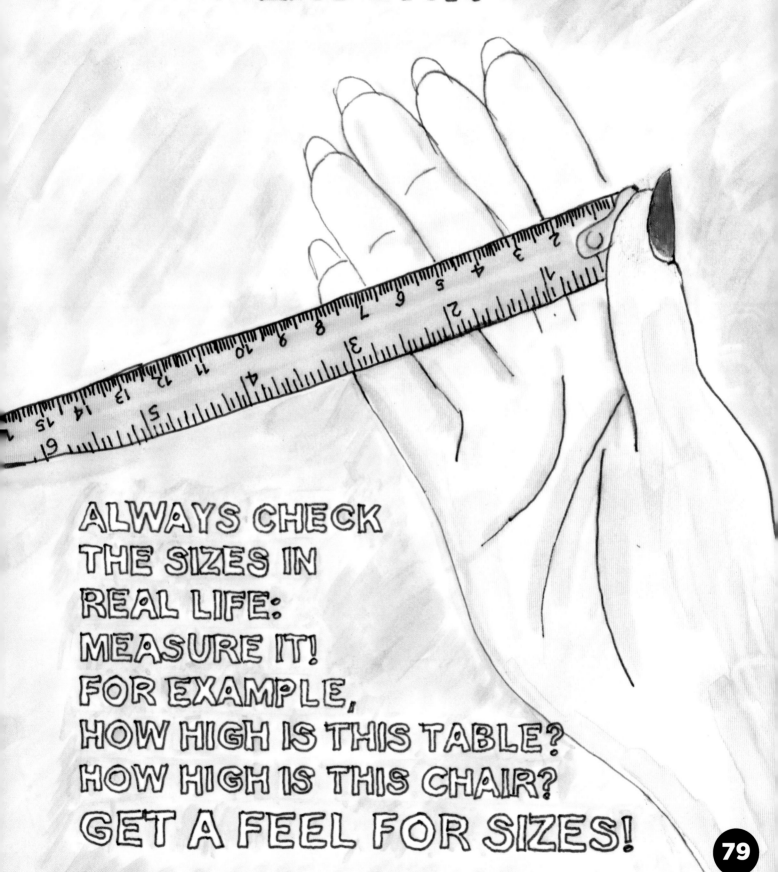

YOU HAVE TO USE THIS TOOL EVERY DAY!

ALWAYS CHECK
THE SIZES IN
REAL LIFE:
MEASURE IT!
FOR EXAMPLE,
HOW HIGH IS THIS TABLE?
HOW HIGH IS THIS CHAIR?
GET A FEEL FOR SIZES!

SIZE MATTERS
STANDARD SIZES ARE DIFFERENT!

1 CM	THICKNESS OF A WOOD FLOOR.	3/8"
2 CM	THICKNESS OF A CABINET DOOR.	1/2"
2.5 CM	THICKNESS OF A TABLE TOP.	1"
5 CM	WIDTH OF A WINDOW FRAME.	2"
12 CM	WIDTH OF A SEPARATION WALL.	4 1/2"
17 CM	RISER HEIGHT OF A STAIR.	7"
30 CM	DEPTH OF A TREAD. LENGTH OF A FOOT. DEPTH OF A BOOKCASE.	12"
40 CM	DEPTH OF A CABINET.	16"
45 CM	SIZE OF A CHAIR: SEATING HEIGHT, WIDTH, DEPTH, AND BACK REST.	18"
60 CM	DEPTH AND WIDTH OF A KITCHEN CABINET, WIDTH OF YOUR SHOULDERS.	24"
76 CM	HEIGHT OF A TABLE.	30"

COMPARE THE STANDARD SIZES IN METRIC AND ENGLISH! THEY ARE DIFFERENT. YOU CANNOT JUST CONVERT THEM. MEMORIZE THEM!

Metric	Description	English
85 CM	HEIGHT OF A BATHROOM VANITY	33"
90 CM	HEIGHT OF A KITCHEN COUNTER. WIDTH OF A KITCHEN CABINET.	36"
100 CM	WIDTH OF A SINGLE BED.	38"
110 CM	HEIGHT OF A BAR TOP.	43"
165 CM	EYE HEIGHT. HORIZON LINE.	5'-6"
200 CM	OPENING HEIGHT OF AN ENTRY DOOR. LENGTH OF A BED.	6'-8"
245 CM	LOW ROOM HEIGHT.	8'
250 CM	ROOM HEIGHT.	8'-4"
275 CM	NICE ROOM HEIGHT.	9'
300 CM	TALL ROOM HEIGHT.	10'
530 CM	CEILING HEIGHT OF A ROOM WITH A MEZZANINE.	17'

© KLICK 07

81

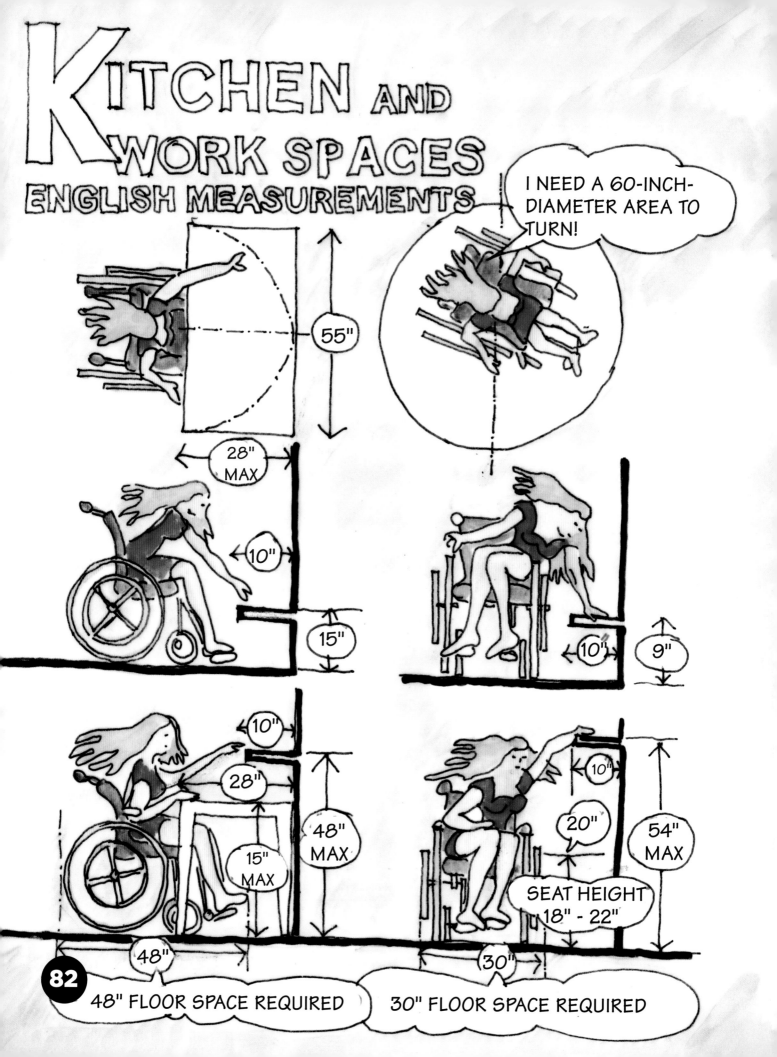

83

METRIC MEASUREMENTS

Bath
English Measurements

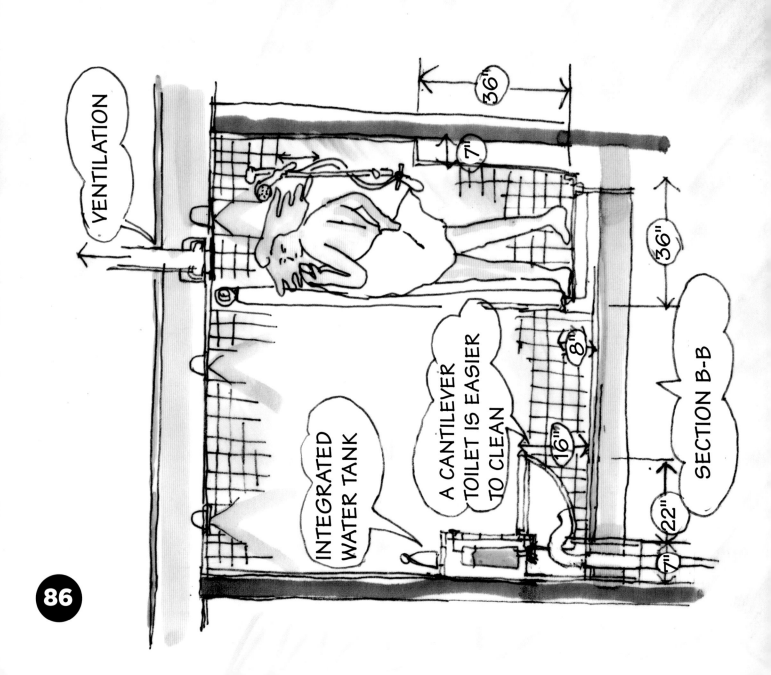

METRIC BATH

SCALE 1:20

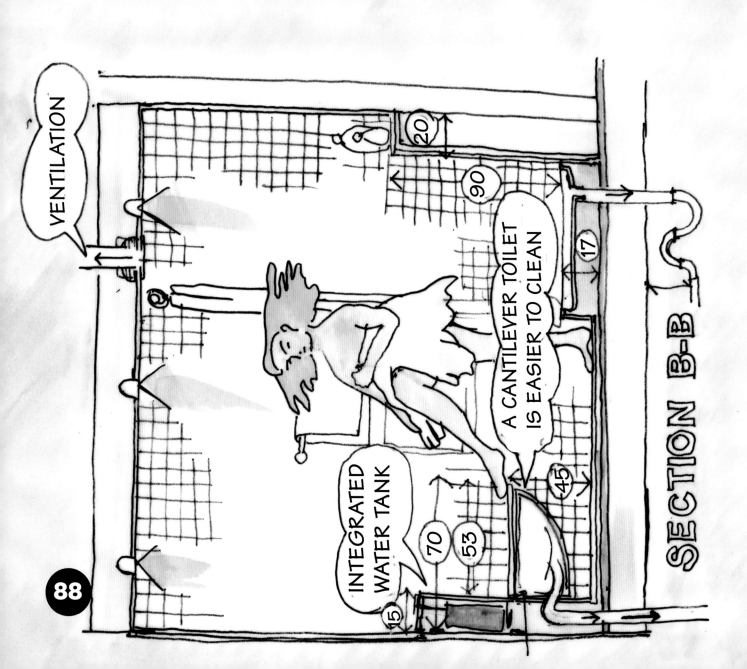

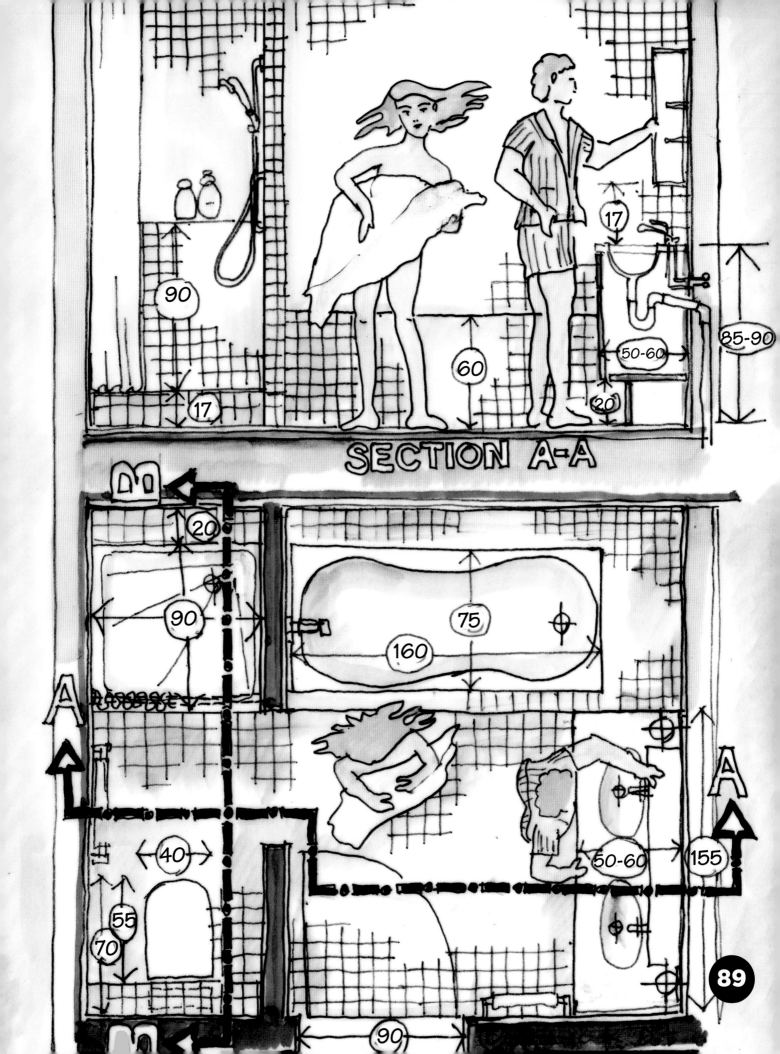

SECTION A-A

89

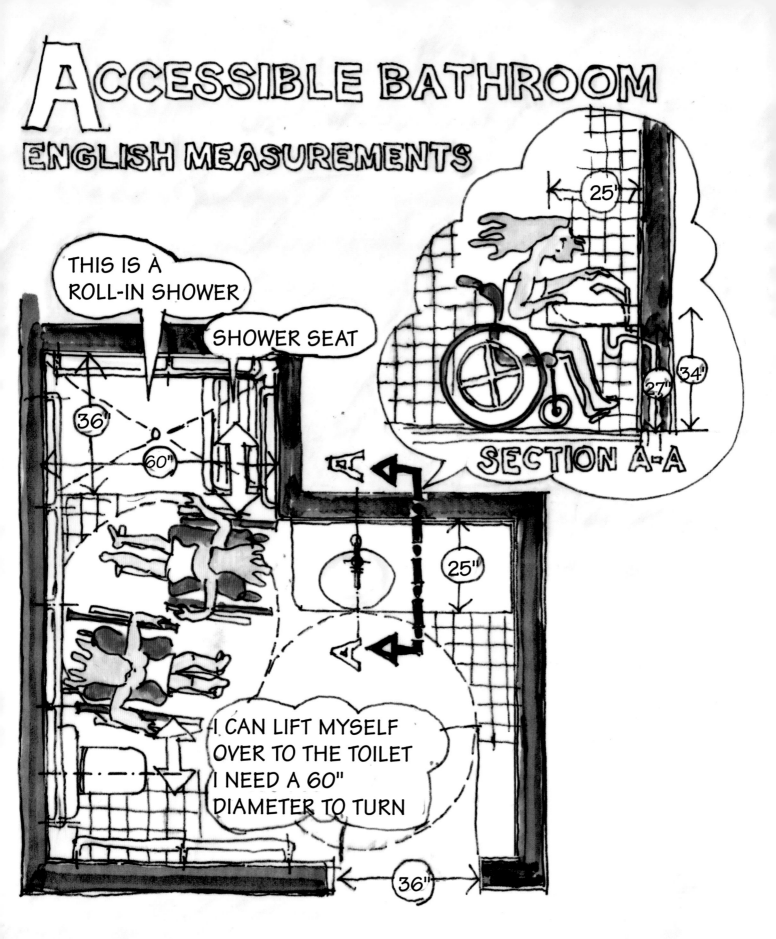

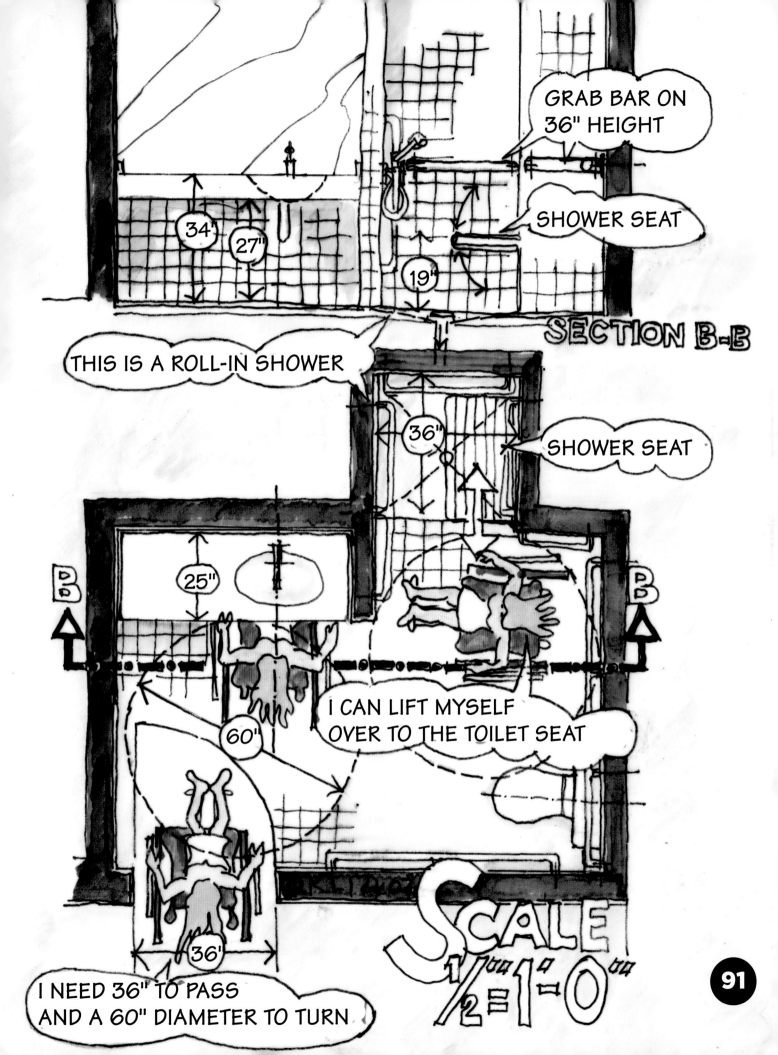

ACCESSIBLE BATHROOM
METRIC MEASUREMENT

SECTION B-B

93

LOUNGE AREA
ENGLISH MEASUREMENTS.
SPACE REQUIRED: 10' X 14'

DINING TABLES
ENGLISH MEASUREMENTS

SCALE: ½" = 1'-0"

TABLE SIZE   8' X 3'
SPACE REQUIRED   14' X 9'

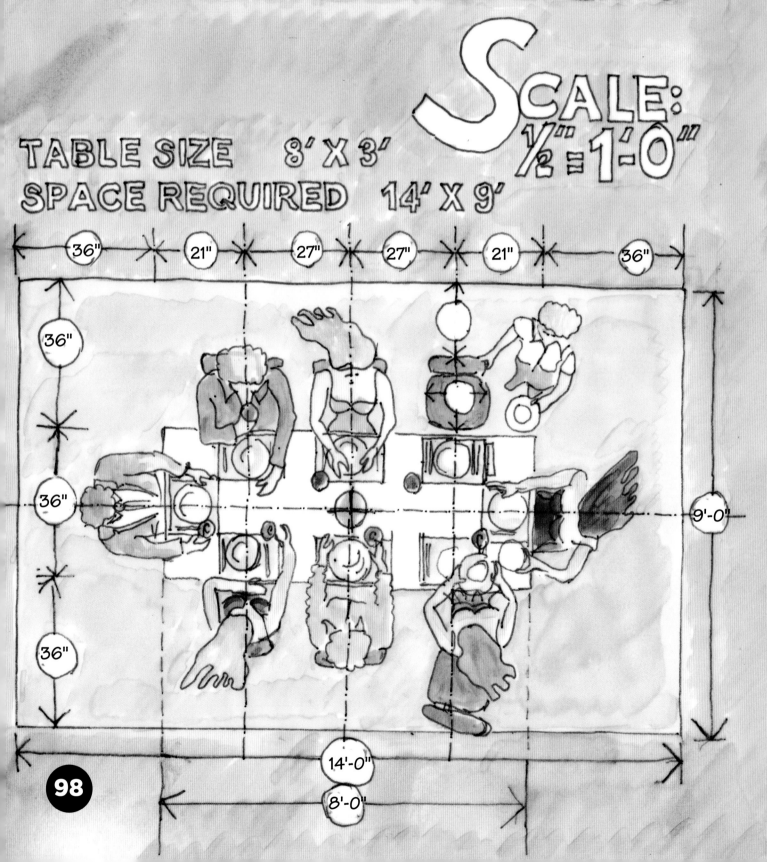

36" 21" 27" 27" 21" 36"

36"

36"

36"

36"

9'-0"

14'-0"

8'-0"

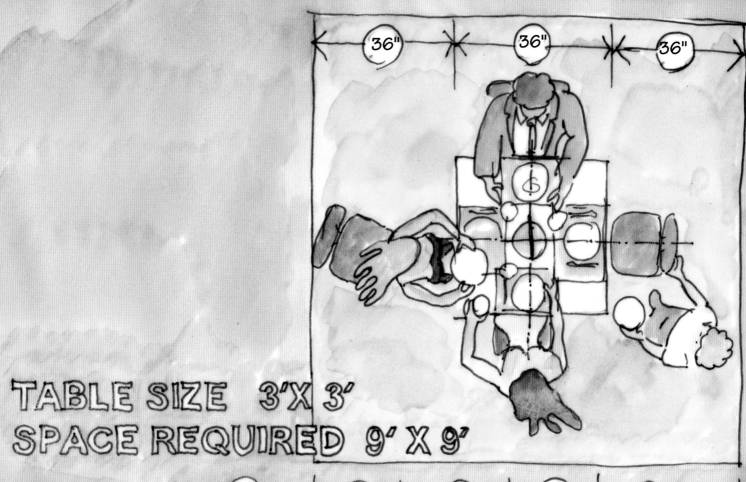

TABLE SIZE 3'X 3'
SPACE REQUIRED 9' X 9'

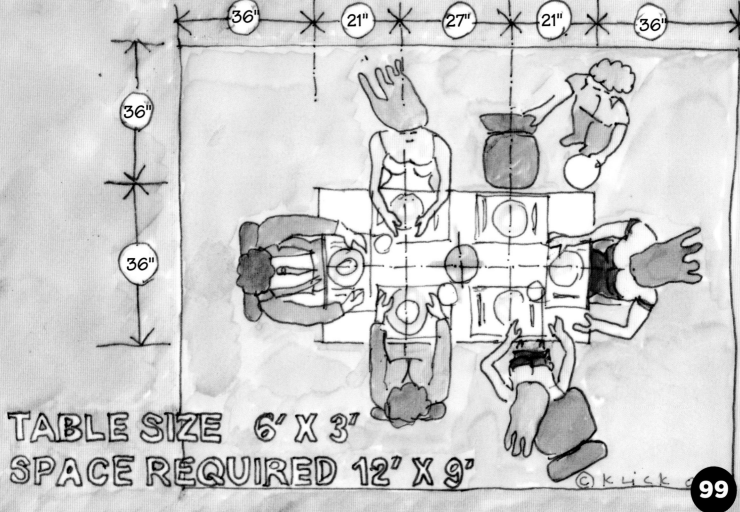

TABLE SIZE 6' X 3'
SPACE REQUIRED 12' X 9'

ENGLISH MEASUREMENTS

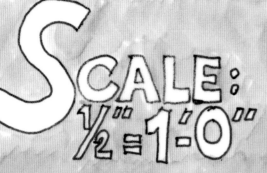

SCALE: ½" = 1'-0"

TABLE SIZE   54" DIAMETER
SPACE REQUIRED 10'-6" DIAMETER

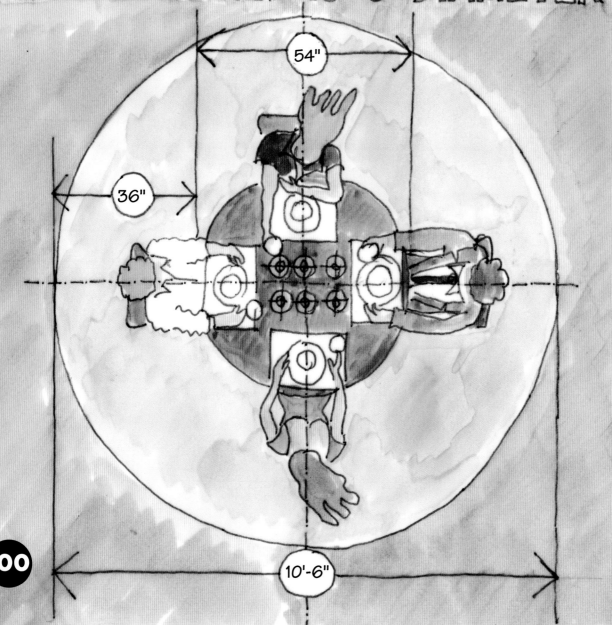

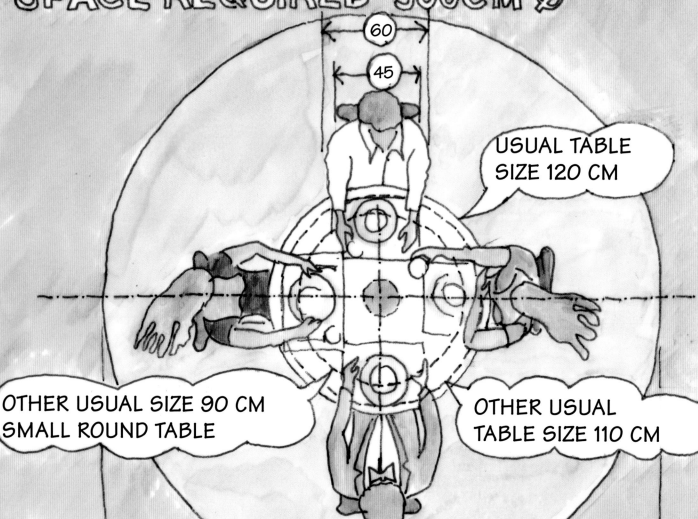

TABLES FROM EUROPE
METRIC
SCALE: 1:20

TABLE SIZE 120CM Ø
SPACE REQUIRED 300CM Ø

SCALE: ½" = 1'-0"

80"

30" × 30"

SPLIT QUEEN

60"

QUEEN

MATTRESS
BOX SPRING
BED FRAME

26"

11"
18"
7"

SPLIT QUEEN

QUEEN

DON'T DISTURB ME...

FOR TWO ADULTS

KING
IS BIGGER BETTER?
DEPENDS ON WHO
IS MAKING THE BED

CALIFORNIA KING
GREAT FOR TALL
GUYS... 84" LONG

FULL LONG
SMALL BED FOR
TWO ADULTS

FULL
TOO SHORT FOR
THE TALL GUYS

107

Beds from Europe

Metric

200

200

90

100

A LITTLE LARGER THEN A TWIN LONG

Scale 1:20

90CM

100CM

20
11
14
45

SMALL BED FOR KIDS

BED FOR ONE ADULT

200 120 140 200

COMPARE TO FULL LONG

120CM 140CM

© kLick 07

NICE SINGLE BED SIZE SMALL BED FOR TWO ADULTS

111

ONE- AND TWO-POINT PERSPECTIVES

CHAPTER 6

ONE-POINT PERSPECTIVE

1

2

3

4

5

6

ALWAYS USE A ONE-POINT PERSPECTIVE WHEN YOU NEED TO SKETCH A ROOM. THIS IS VERY EASY, QUICK TO CONSTRUCT, AND WILL IMPRESS YOUR CLIENTS. YOU WILL NEED TO SHOW YOUR CLIENT A 3-D IMAGE TO SELL YOUR IDEAS. JUST FOLLOW THESE TIPS:

- STAND PARALLEL TO THE FRONT AND BACK WALL
- USE THE GRID TO PLACE THE FURNITURE
- REMEMBER THAT ALL HORIZONTAL LINES NEED TO BE PARALLEL TO YOUR STANDING POINT
- ALL HORIZONTAL-DEPTH LINES EXTEND TO THE VANISHING POINT
- ALL VERTICAL LINES STAY VERTICAL

IT IS VERY IMPORTANT TO MAINTAIN *GOOD SKETCHING SKILLS.* A ONE-POINT PERSPECTIVE IS A FAST SOLUTION, ESPECIALLY IF YOU DO NOT HAVE TIME OR A COMPUTER HANDY. ALWAYS CARRY PENCILS WITH YOU AND SKETCH EVERYTHING! YOU WILL ALWAYS NEED A 3-DIMENSIONAL IMAGE FOR YOUR CLIENT TO SELL HIM OR HER YOUR IDEAS. A ONE-POINT PERSPECTIVE SKETCH IS A FAST SOLUTION. EVERYONE CAN SKETCH. IT IS EASY; YOU JUST HAVE TO KNOW HOW TO DO IT.

@KLICK 07

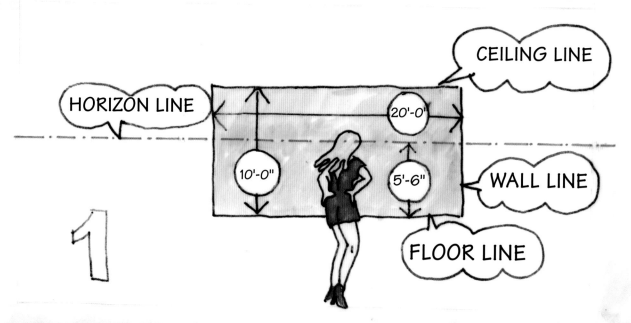

1

START WITH AN ELEVATION OF THE BACK WALL IN SCALE. THIS ONE IS IN A 1/8"-1' SCALE SIMILAR TO 1:100 IN METRIC. DRAW THE HORIZON LINE ON FROM YOUR EYE HEIGHT ON 5'-6", OR 165CM HEIGHT IN METRIC, FROM THE FLOOR LINE.

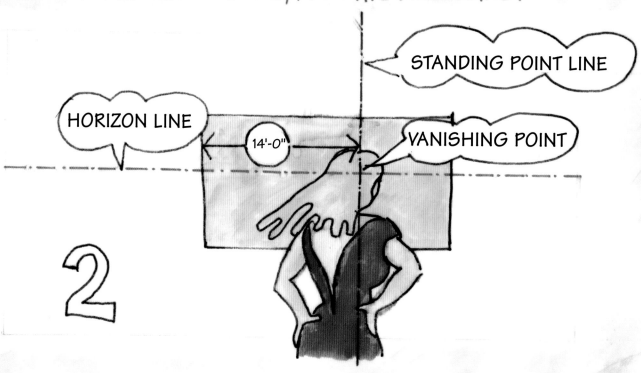

2

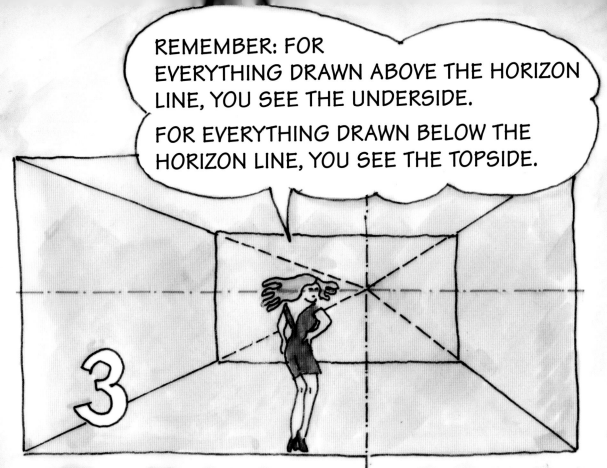

REMEMBER: FOR EVERYTHING DRAWN ABOVE THE HORIZON LINE, YOU SEE THE UNDERSIDE.

FOR EVERYTHING DRAWN BELOW THE HORIZON LINE, YOU SEE THE TOPSIDE.

CREATE THE ROOM LINES:
EXTEND THE LINES FROM THE VANISHING POINT THROUGH THE CORNERS OF THE ROOM ON YOUR ELEVATION. YOUR ROOM IS DONE!

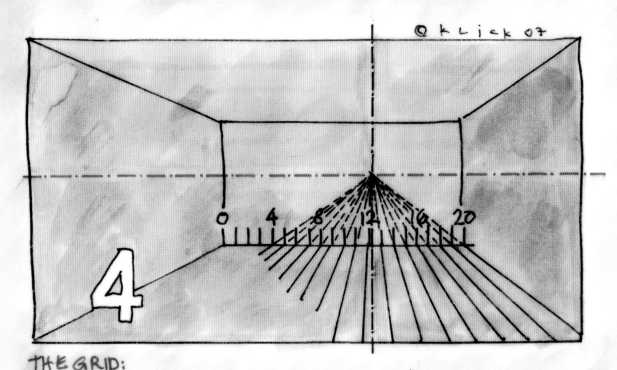

© klick 07

THE GRID:
CREATE A 1-FOOT SCALE OR A 10-CM SCALE ON THE FLOOR LINE. EXTEND LINES FROM THE VANISHING POINT THROUGH EACH MARK ON THE SCALE LINE ACROSS THE FLOOR.

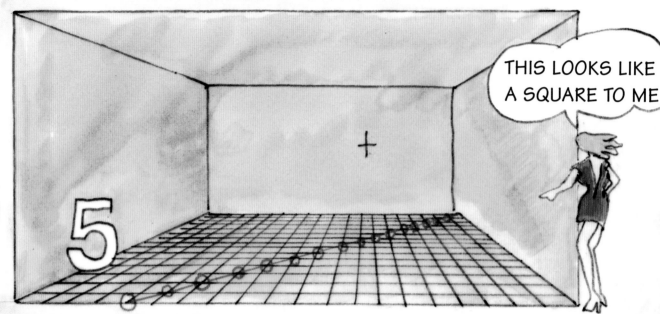

DEPTH:

EYEBALL A SQUARE IN FRONT OF THE FLOOR ON THE EXTENDED SCALE LINES. TO DEVELOP THE 1-FOOT DEPTH LINES, DRAW A DIAGONAL LINE FROM THE FRONT LEFT CORNER THROUGH THE BACK RIGHT CORNER OF THE SQUARE. EXTEND THIS DIAGONAL LINE ACROSS THE ENTIRE FLOOR. EACH LINE IS 1-FT OR 25 CM DEEP.

THE PLACEMENT OF PEOPLE IN THE PERSPECTIVE GIVES SCALE TO THE SPACE AND INDICATES DEPTH. ALWAYS PLACE PEOPLE'S EYE LEVEL ON THE HORIZON LINE (EXCEPT WHEN YOU DRAW CHILDREN). THE SMALLER YOU DRAW THE PERSON, THE FARTHER AWAY HE OR SHE WILL APPEAR.

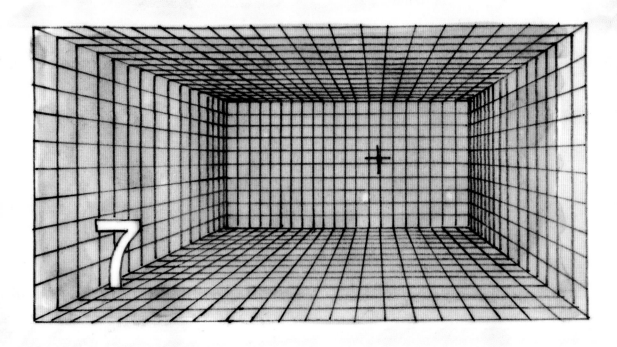

EXTEND THE GRID TO THE WALLS AND THE CEILING. YOU CAN ALSO USE A TEMPLATE.

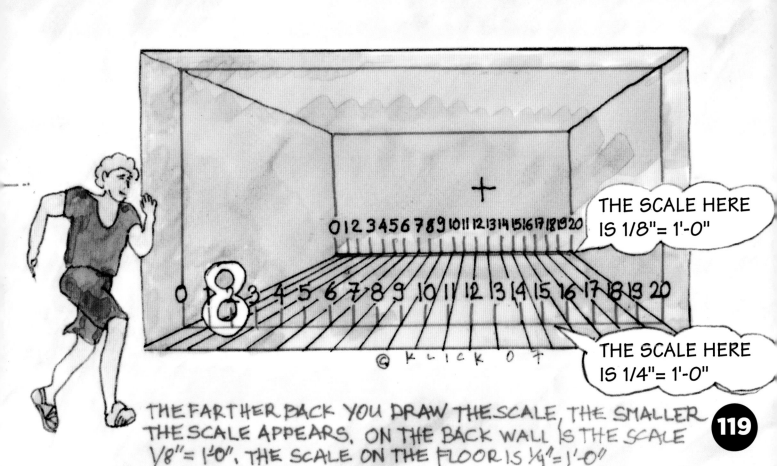

THE SCALE HERE IS 1/8"= 1'-0"

THE SCALE HERE IS 1/4"= 1'-0"

THE FARTHER BACK YOU DRAW THE SCALE, THE SMALLER THE SCALE APPEARS. ON THE BACK WALL IS THE SCALE 1/8"= 1'-0", THE SCALE ON THE FLOOR IS 1/4"= 1'-0"

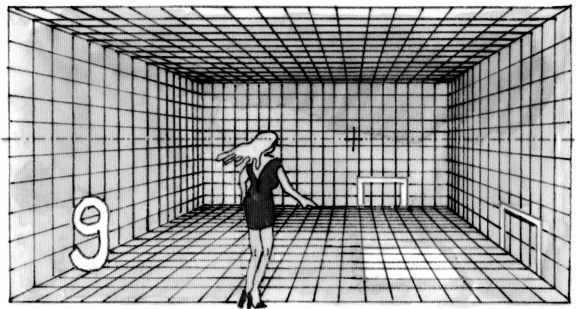

9

PLACE YOUR FURNITURE IN THE ROOM:
DRAW YOUR ELEVATIONS ON THE GRID OF THE BACK WALL
AND A SIDE WALL. EXTEND THE LINES FROM THE WALLS ON
THE FLOOR IN THE ROOM.

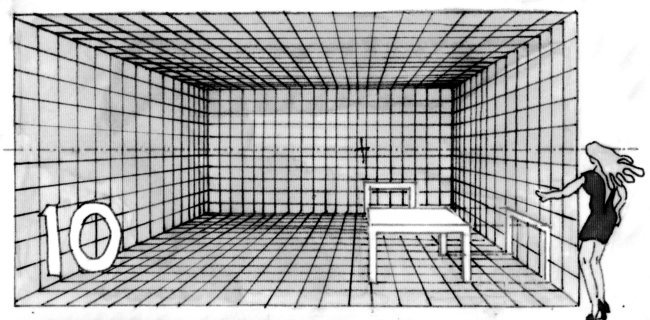

10

ELEVATE THE HEIGHT OF THE FURNITURE. THE DIMENSIONS
OF THIS TABLE ARE 4'-0" X 4'-0" X 2'-6"
REMEMBER:
ALL VERTICAL LINES REMAIN VERTICAL AND ALL
HORIZONTAL LINES REMAIN HORIZONTAL!

DRAWING A TABLE WITH A 45° ANGLE TO THE ROOM:
DRAW THE TABLE'S FLOOR PLAN AND THE ELEVATION ON
THE BACK WALL. DRAW THE ELEVATION OF THE TABLE ON
A SIDE WALL. EXTEND THE LINES ON THE FLOOR INTO THE
ROOM. CREATE TWO NEW VANISHING POINTS (THE LEFT
AND THE RIGHT VANISHING POINTS) BY EXTENDING THE
LINES ON THE HORIZON LINE.

© KLICK 07

ELEVATE THE HEIGHT OF THE TABLE, THE DIMENSIONS OF
THIS TABLE ARE 4'-6" X 4'-6" X 2'-6"
REMEMBER: THE HORIZONTAL LINES END ON THE NEW
VANISHING POINTS THAT YOU CREATED. KEEP VERTICAL
LINES VERTICAL!

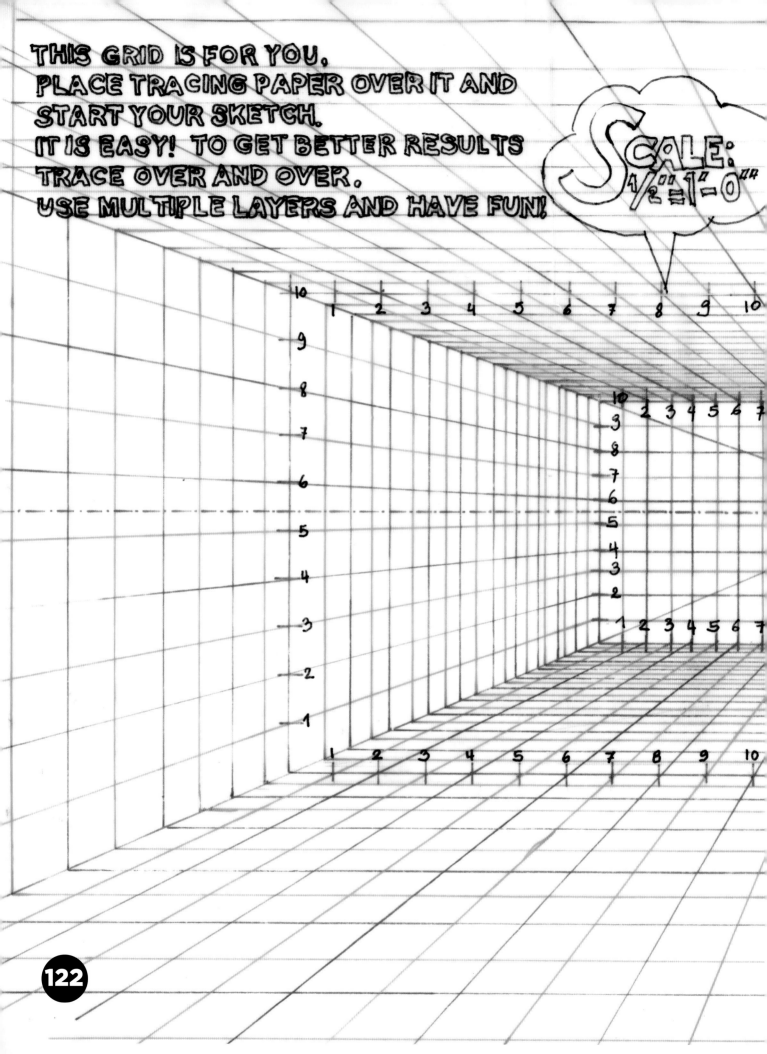

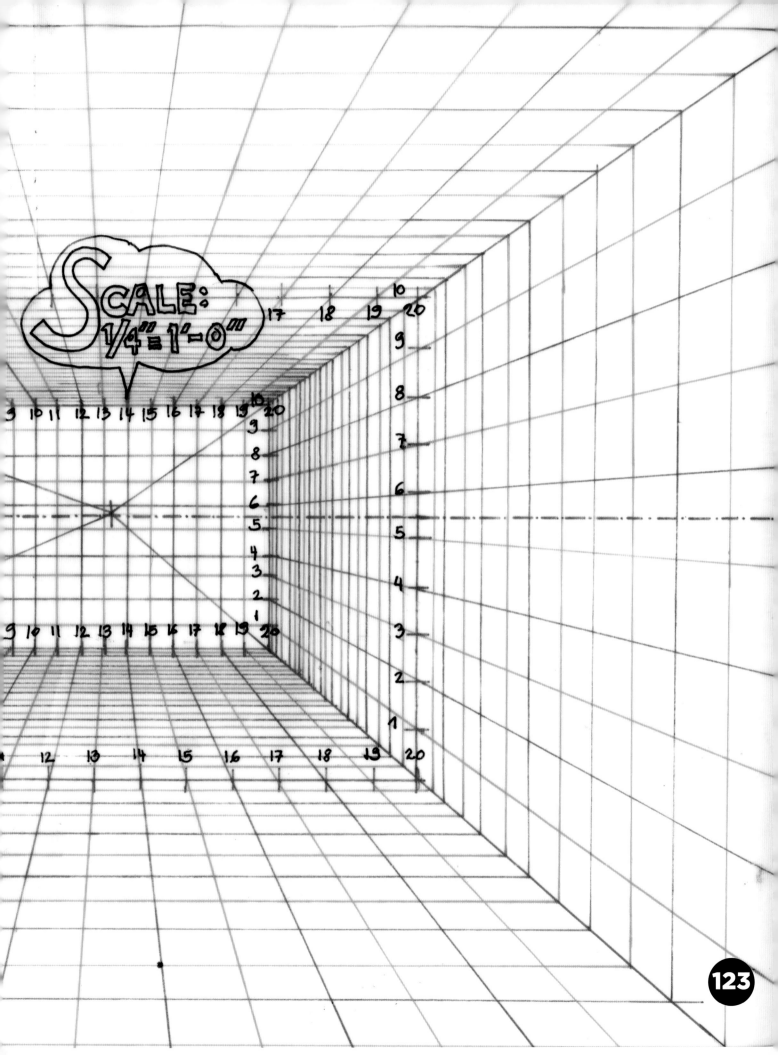

SCALE: 1/4" = 1'-0"

123

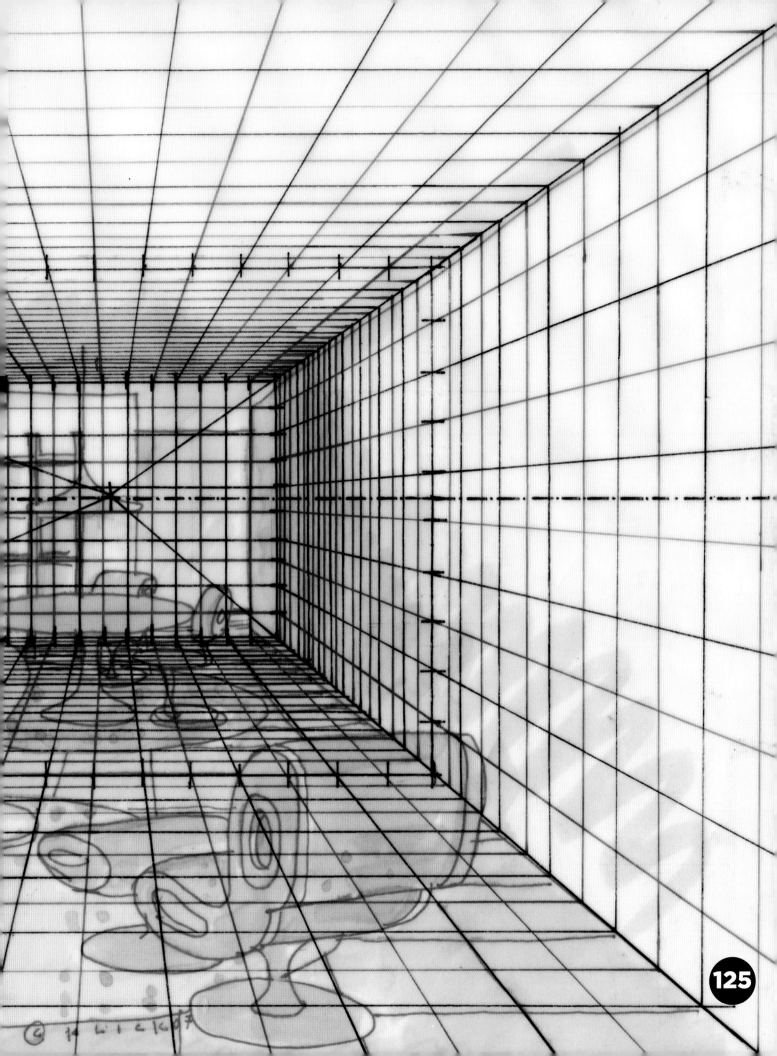

125

127

TWO-POINT PERSPECTIVE

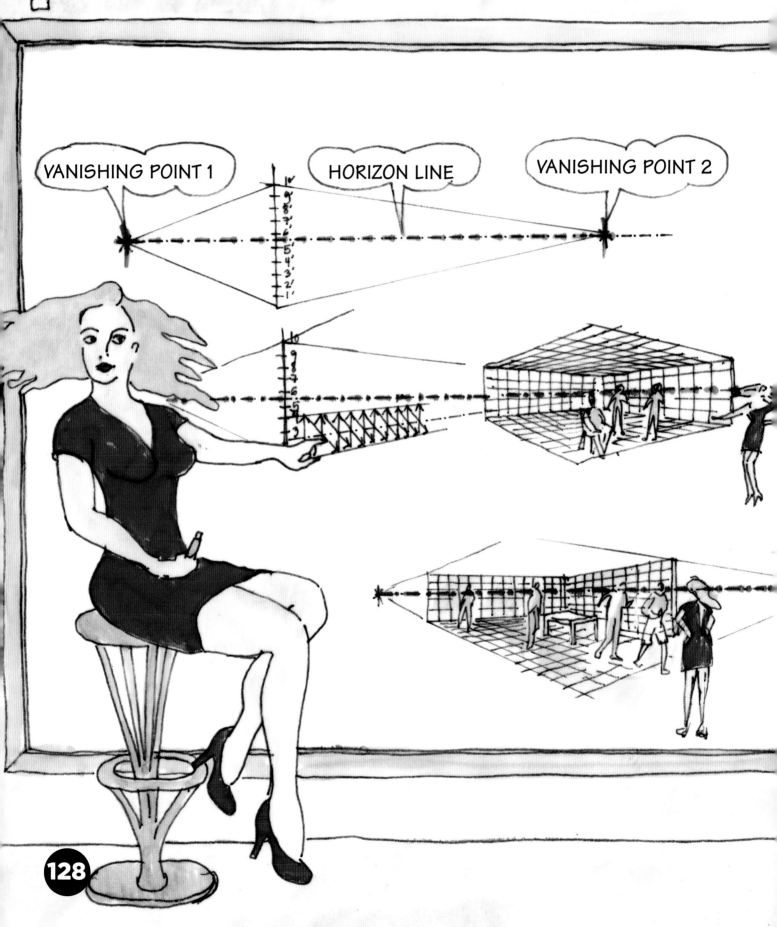

VANISHING POINT 1

HORIZON LINE

VANISHING POINT 2

A TWO-POINT PERSPECTIVE IS VALUABLE WHEN YOU HAVE TO SHOW FURNITURE—SUCH AS CHAIRS, DESKS, OR KITCHENS—OR WHEN VIEWING PARTS OF A ROOM INSTEAD OF A WHOLE ROOM. TWO-POINT PERSPECTIVES ARE SLIGHTLY MORE COMPLICATED TO DRAW THAN ONE-POINT PERSPECTIVES BECAUSE YOU ARE STANDING ON AN ANGLE TO THE ROOM INSTEAD OF PARALLEL TO THE FRONT AND BACK WALLS. WITH A GRID, HOWEVER, IT IS VERY EASY!

© KLICK 07

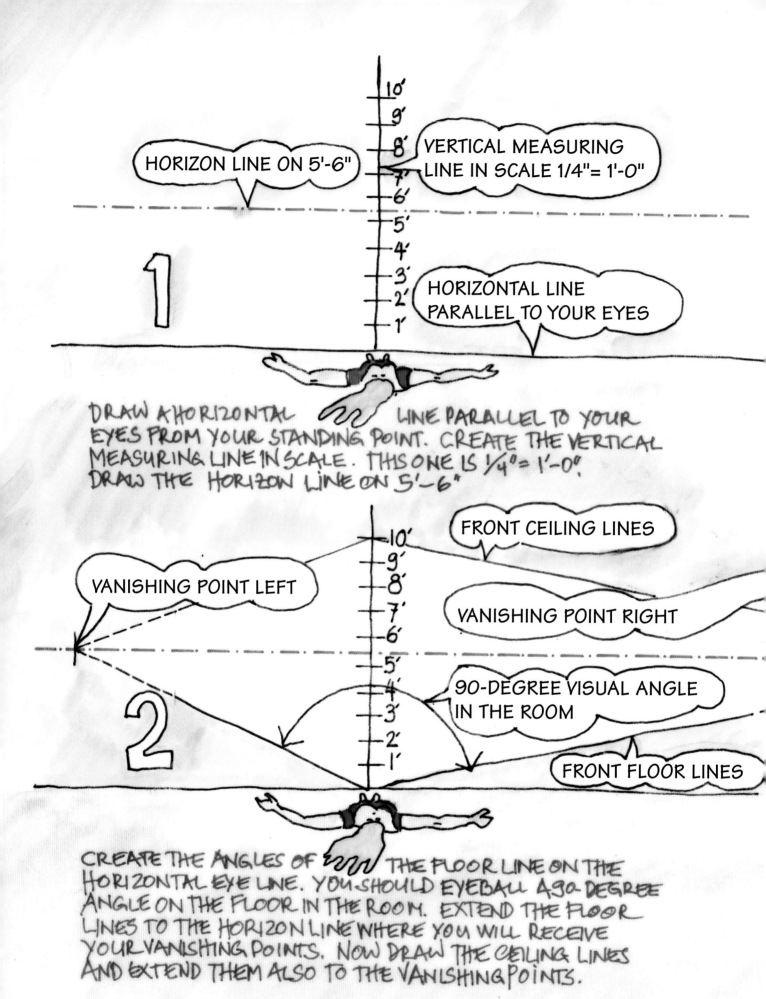

DRAW A HORIZONTAL LINE PARALLEL TO YOUR EYES FROM YOUR STANDING POINT. CREATE THE VERTICAL MEASURING LINE IN SCALE. THIS ONE IS 1/4"= 1'-0". DRAW THE HORIZON LINE ON 5'-6".

CREATE THE ANGLES OF THE FLOOR LINE ON THE HORIZONTAL EYE LINE. YOU SHOULD EYEBALL A 90 DEGREE ANGLE ON THE FLOOR IN THE ROOM. EXTEND THE FLOOR LINES TO THE HORIZON LINE WHERE YOU WILL RECEIVE YOUR VANISHING POINTS. NOW DRAW THE CEILING LINES AND EXTEND THEM ALSO TO THE VANISHING POINTS.

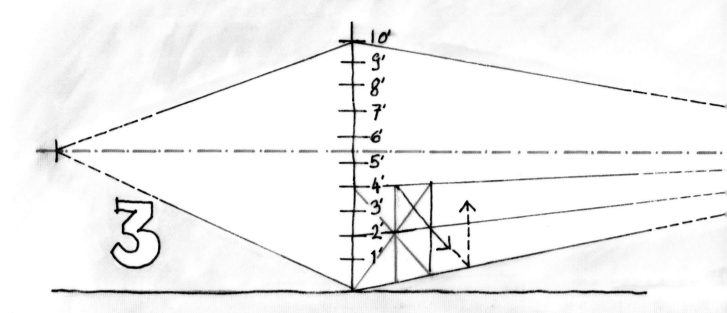

EYEBALL A 4'-0" SQUARE WITH THE HELP OF YOUR VERTICAL
SCALE LINE. DIVIDE IT WITH THE HELP OF A LINE AT A
HEIGHT OF 2'-0", AND EXTEND IT TO THE VANISHING POINT.
DIVIDE THE SQUARE TO A VISUAL HALF WITH
TWO-DIAGONAL LINES.

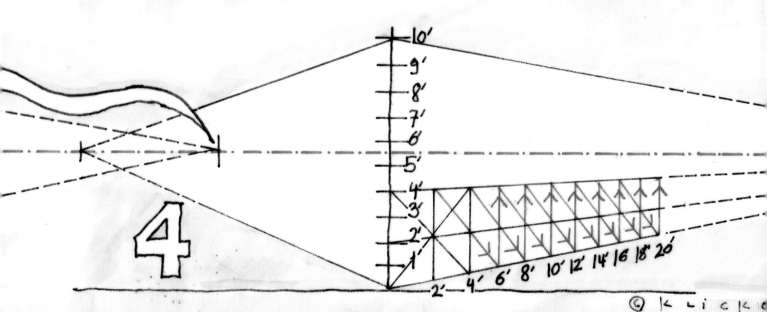

REPEAT THIS PROCEDURE AND YOU WILL
RECEIVE A 2'-0" MEASURING SCALE THAT
REDUCES THE FARTHER BACK IT GOES.

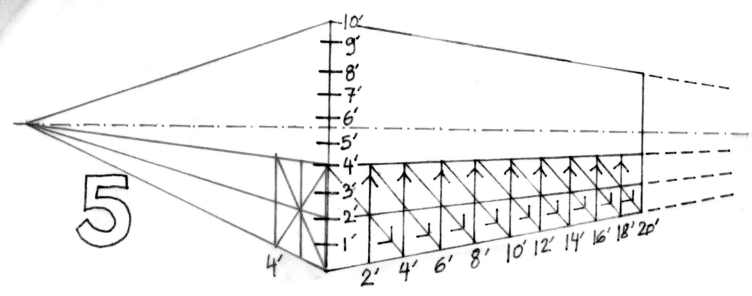

5   EYEBALL THE 4'-0" SQUARE ON THE LEFT WALL

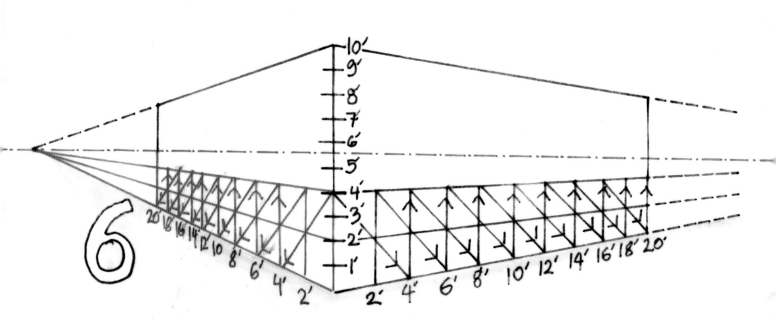

6   NOW, REPEAT THE SAME PROCEDURE...

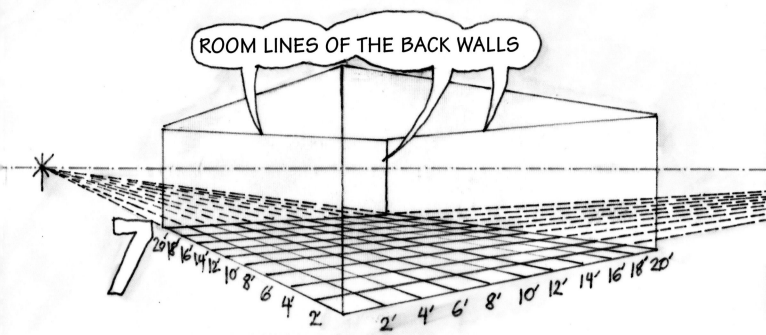

ROOM LINES OF THE BACK WALLS

DRAW THE GRID ON THE FLOOR AND DRAW THE ROOM LINES OF THE BACK WALLS.

IF YOU LIKE YOU CAN DRAW THE GRID ON THE WALLS AND THE CEILING TOO.

133

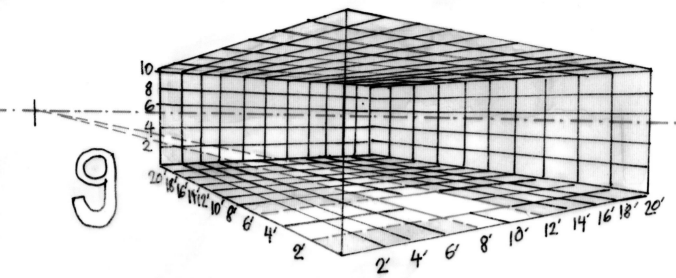

9

WHEN THE FURNITURE IN THE ROOM IS PLACED IN A DIFFERENT ANGLE TO THE ROOM, YOU HAVE TO CHANGE THE VANISHING POINTS FOR THE FURNITURE. REMEMBER: THE VANISHING POINTS ARE ALWAYS ON THE HORIZON LINE ON BOTH THE ONE- AND TWO-POINT PERSPECTIVES.

10

TO MEASURE HEIGHT, COUNT THE SQUARES ON THE WALLS OF THE GRID.

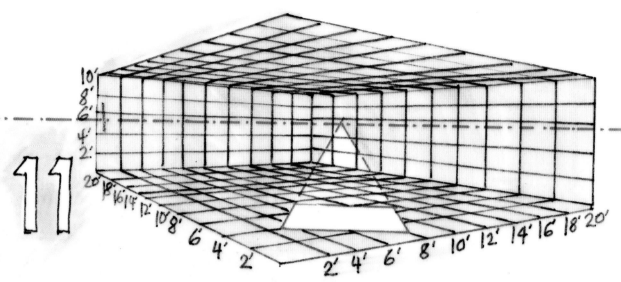

11

WHEN THE FURNITURE IN THE ROOM IS PLACED IN A
DIFFERENT ANGLE TO THE ROOM, YOU HAVE TO CHANGE
THE VANISHING POINTS FOR THE FURNITURE. REMEMBER:
THE VANISHING POINTS ARE ALWAYS ON THE HORIZON LINE
ON BOTH THE ONE- AND TWO-POINT PERSPECTIVES.

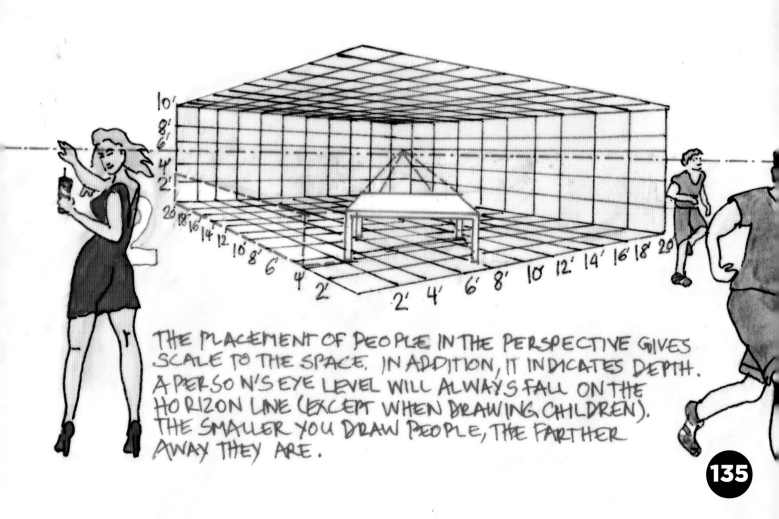

THE PLACEMENT OF PEOPLE IN THE PERSPECTIVE GIVES
SCALE TO THE SPACE. IN ADDITION, IT INDICATES DEPTH.
A PERSON'S EYE LEVEL WILL ALWAYS FALL ON THE
HORIZON LINE (EXCEPT WHEN DRAWING CHILDREN).
THE SMALLER YOU DRAW PEOPLE, THE FARTHER
AWAY THEY ARE.

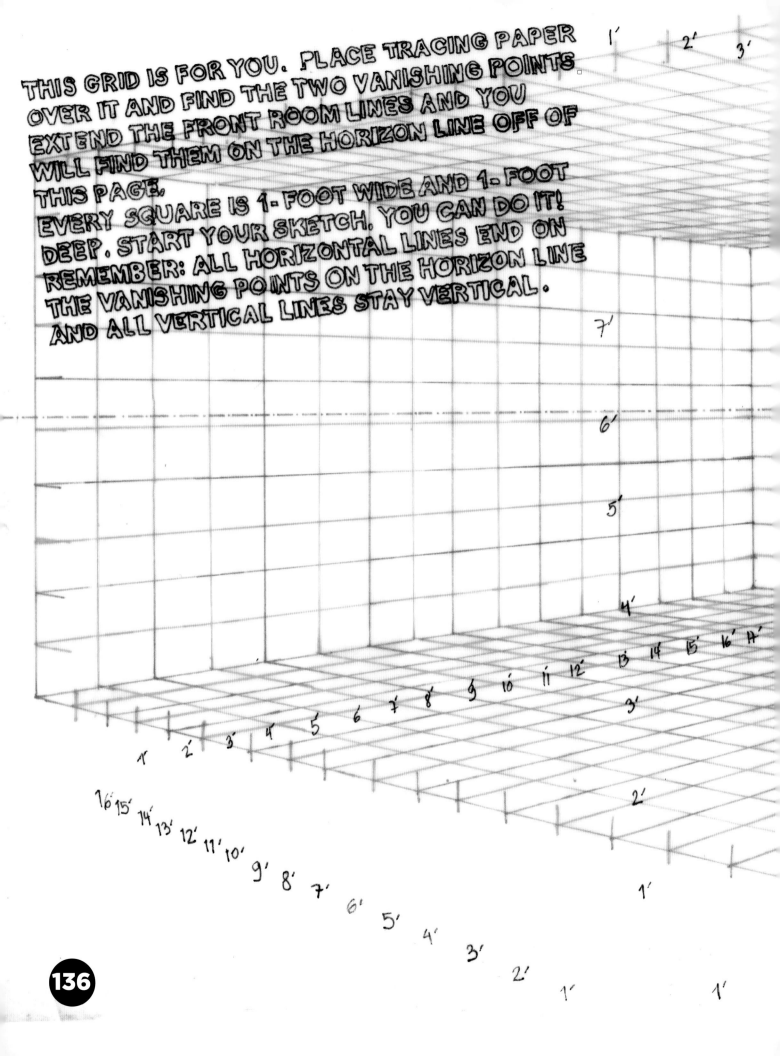

THIS GRID IS FOR YOU. PLACE TRACING PAPER OVER IT AND FIND THE TWO VANISHING POINTS. EXTEND THE FRONT ROOM LINES AND YOU WILL FIND THEM ON THE HORIZON LINE OFF OF THIS PAGE.

EVERY SQUARE IS 1-FOOT WIDE AND 1-FOOT DEEP. START YOUR SKETCH. YOU CAN DO IT! REMEMBER: ALL HORIZONTAL LINES END ON THE VANISHING POINTS ON THE HORIZON LINE AND ALL VERTICAL LINES STAY VERTICAL.

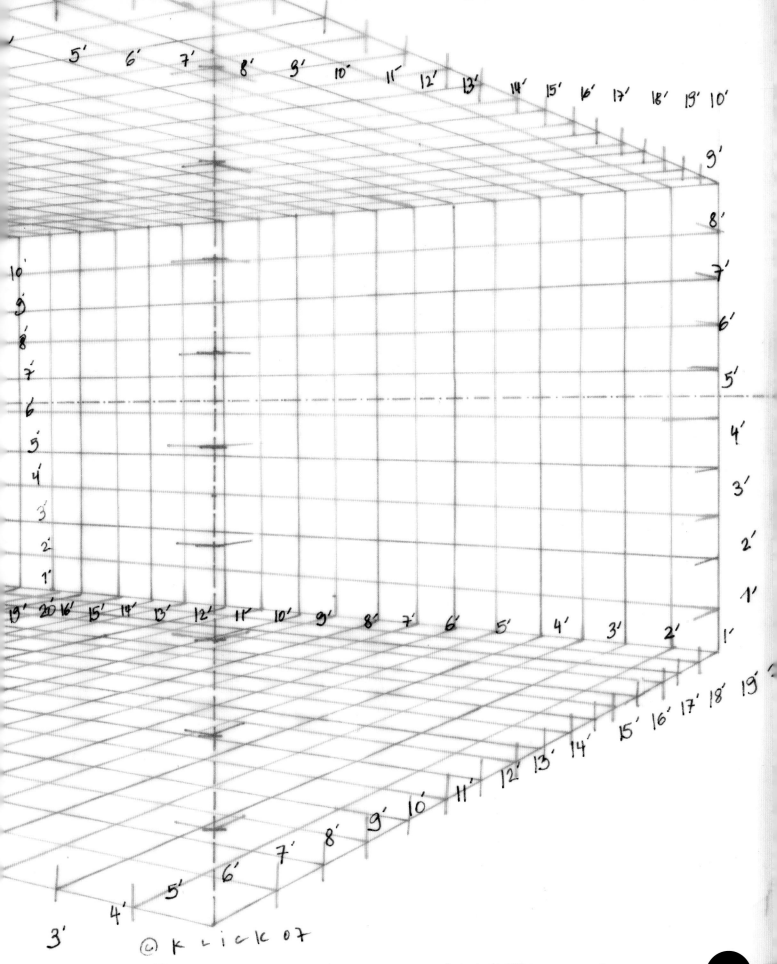

© Klick 07

137

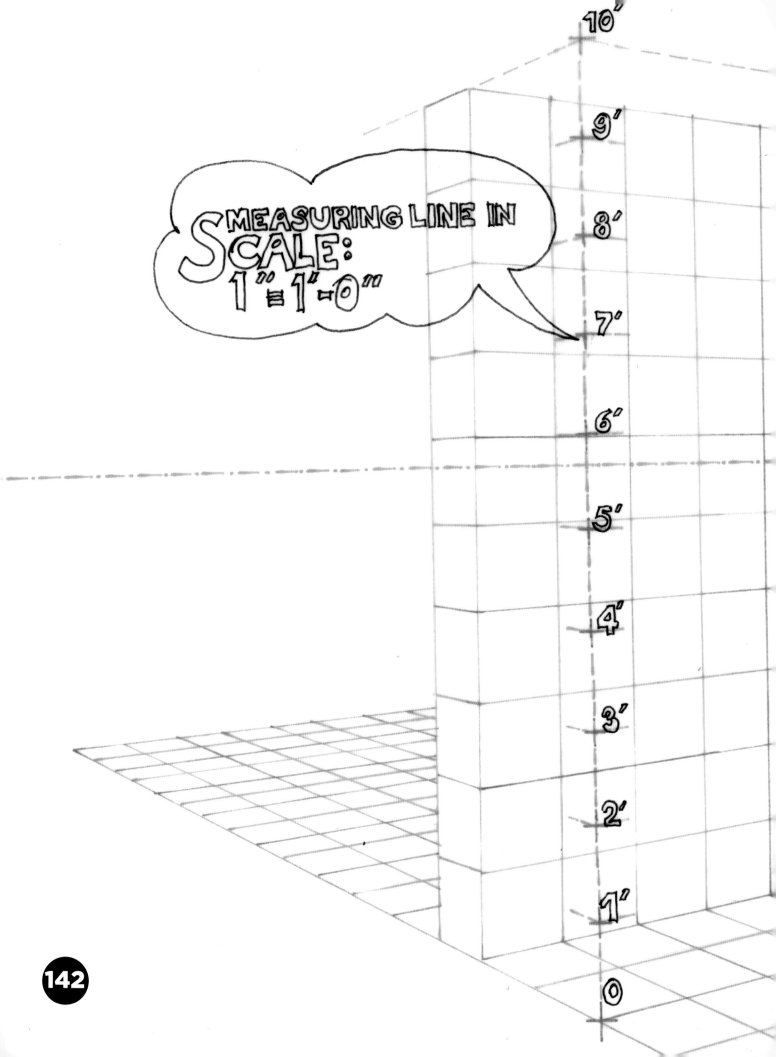

142

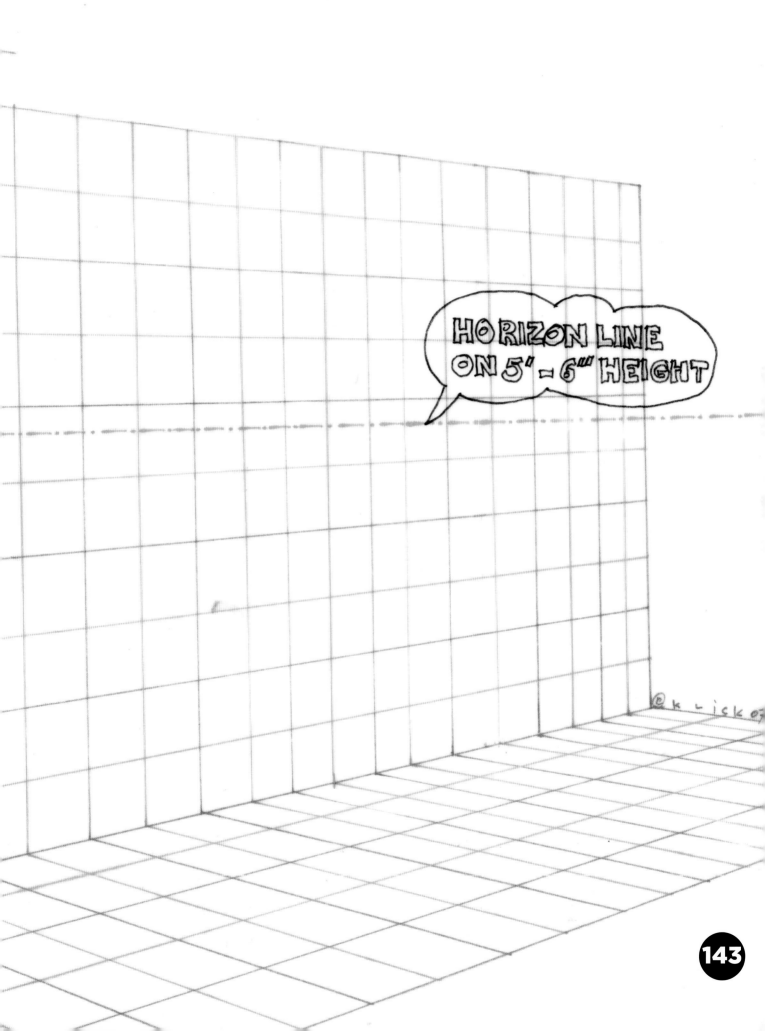

143

145

STAIRS

CHAPTER 7

STAIRS

THE STAIR IS AN IMPORTANT ELEMENT IN YOUR PRO-JECT. IT CAN BE AN ESSENTIAL DESIGN ELEMENT.

START EARLY. START WITH ONE SECTION. FIND OUT THE HEIGHT BETWEEN THE TWO FINISHED FLOORS.

FIRE ESCAPES ARE LIFESAVERS. ALWAYS USE THE LOCAL REQUIREMENTS AND BUILDING CODES.

SCALE: 1/8" = 1'-0"

© KLICK 07

149

TAKE THE HEIGHT FROM THE FINISHED FLOOR TO THE NEXT LEVEL FINISHED FLOOR AND TRANSFER THIS HEIGHT INTO INCHES.

DIVIDE THIS HEIGHT WITH THE ESTIMATED RISER HEIGHT OF 7".

ROUND THE RESULT UP OR DOWN TO GET THE NUMBER OF RISERS YOU NEED.

DIVIDE THE HEIGHT BETWEEN THE TWO FLOORS WITH THE NUMBER OF RISERS AND GET THE PRECISE HEIGHT OF EACH RISER. ROUND THIS DIMENSION UP OR DOWN WITH AN ACCEPTABLE TOLERANCE.

THIS STAIR HAS 19 RISERS AND 18 TREADS.

A TREAD HAS TO HAVE ENOUGH SPACE FOR YOUR FOOT, SO ITS SIZE IS ABOUT ONE-FOOT DEEP!

THE STAIR FORMULA:
2 X RISER + 1 X TREAD = 25"
OR 63CM.
THIS STAIR HAS:
2 X 6.95" + 12" = 25.90"

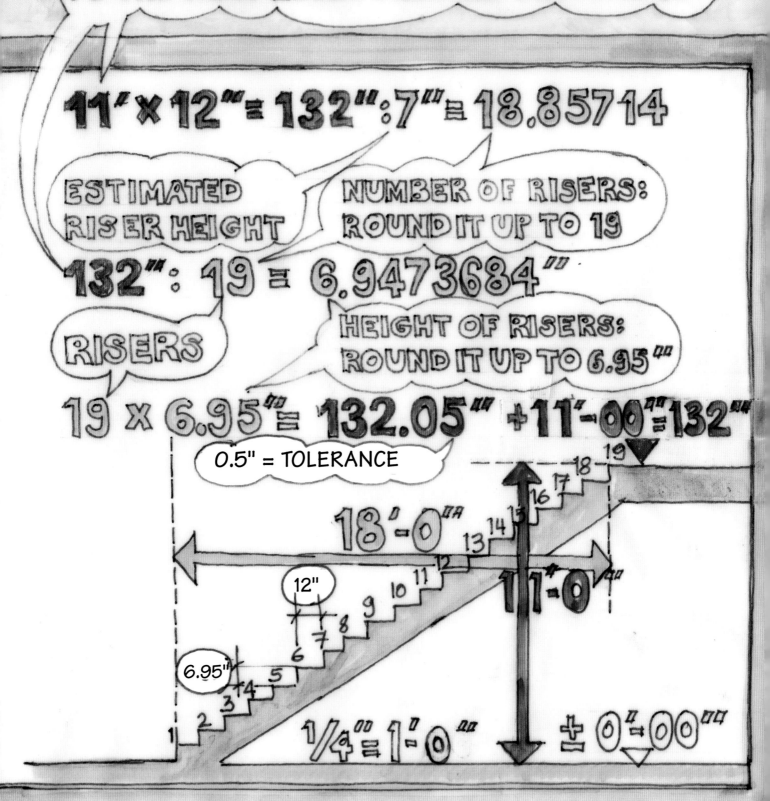

155

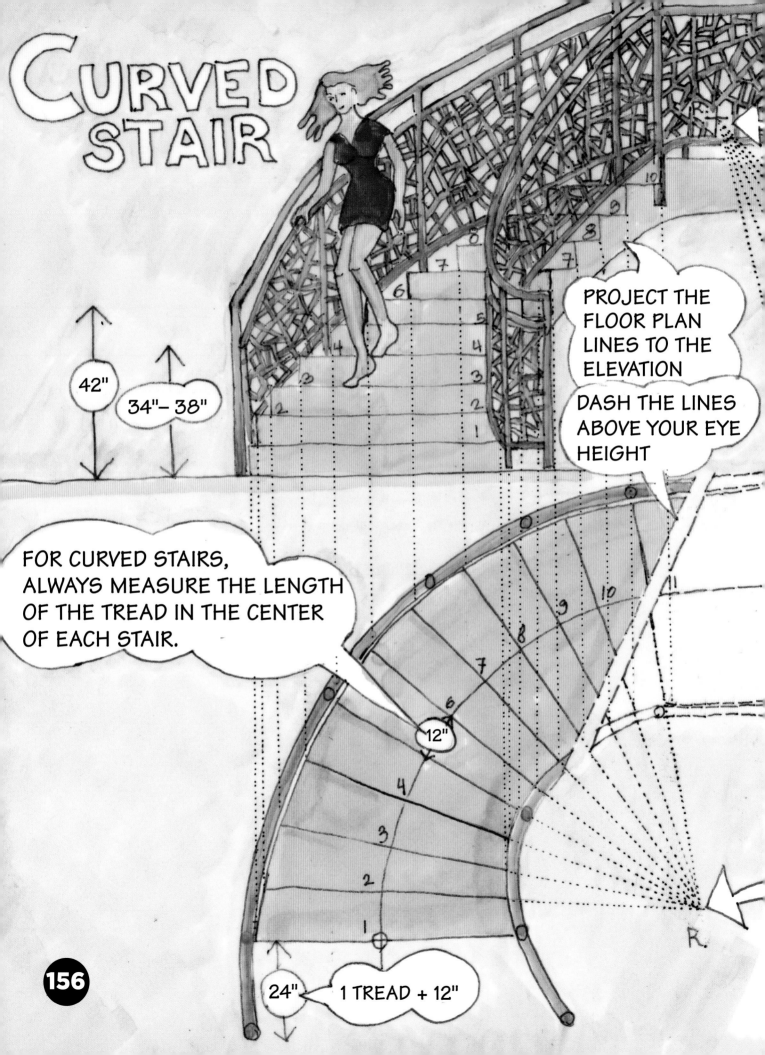

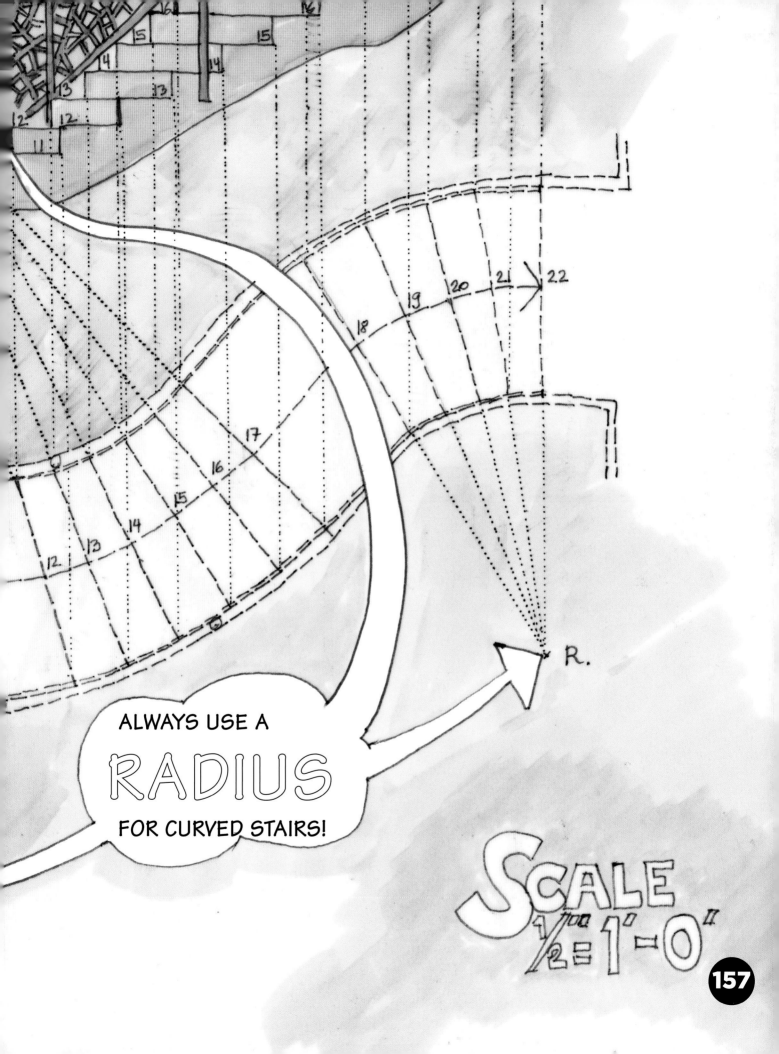

IDENTIFYING
COLOR

CHAPTER 8

In general, we are afraid of color. We fear that we will misuse color and damage our image. As a designer, you must get over your fear. Color is a friend, not an enemy. Acquaint yourself with color. Study it. Surround yourself with it. Research it. We cannot exist without color. It is a part of life. Nature is full of color. In understanding it, all fear dissipates.

Choosing colors of clothing relates closely to interior design. For example, you may ask yourself, "What should I wear today? Blue jeans or a black dress?" For the last 20 years, a friend of mine has worn only black, including his socks and underwear. Because of this, he creates a very strong image and identity for himself. Every day we get to decide. Which color concept will it be today?

A *concept* is the creation of rules brought about by possibilities and their related results. When getting dressed, we make choices based on our body types, complexions, and eye and hair colors. For example, when Tina wears a blue blouse, it matches her blue eyes, which makes them appear more vivid. A beige skirt with a beige jacket matches her blond hair and tanned skin. She may also wear brown shoes and a brown belt as accessories. For jewelry, gold earrings, a gold necklace, and a gold watch can be used for accents.

Similar to getting dressed, an interior designer dresses a room with colors. An interior designer should first ask: "What are the givens—dimensions, windows, location, view, and room height; what do we have to work with?" The next questions should be: "What kind of client do we have? What is the theme?" For example, is there an existing floor? Can we take it out? Will the same floor be used or a new one installed? We may need to preserve it because the client likes it. What about the walls and ceiling? Is there a high ceiling?

The answers to these questions will determine decisions. The decisions will lead to a color and contrast concept—just like Tina's blue eyes, blonde hair, and clothes. If we do not know what our client likes, we need to do research. What does he/she wear? What car does he/she drive? Where does the client like to go on vacation? Where does he/she work and live? Explore your client's world and get acquainted with his or her life.

In communicating with clients, I've found that the client likes what his or her partner likes. I've been able to find out a lot through a partner. For example, "Mr. Smith doesn't really care about the kitchen because I do all of the cooking. But I've always dreamed of having a blue kitchen with chrome steel sinks and counter tops."

Another client likes blue, the ocean, seashells, sand, fishing, silver, chrome, and fine dining. Get the picture?

Say, for instance, that you need to design a

house. Mom wants a blue living and dining room and each child wants a different colored room. Where do you start?

First, create a concept. It can be a colored concept, with various colors, but again, create a clear concept that utilizes contrasts. Colors are personal matters of taste, and clients have diverse personalities, but make sure your contrasts are absolutely correct. Marry the contrasts with whatever colors you select. Observations will assist you greatly in learning the likes and dislikes of your clients and their personalities. View, watch, observe, and research. Once you find the answers, the concept clicks into place. Then you can make decisions.

Subjective tastes cannot suffice for the solution of all color problems. Knowledge of objective principles is essential to the correct evaluation and use of colors. Study and know your colors. When a customer is looking for a certain hue, he or she needs to know what other colors may strengthen, weaken, or otherwise modify it. Designers sometimes tend to be guided by their own subjective color propensities. This may lead to misunderstandings and disputes, where one subjective judgment collides with another. For the solution of many problems, however, there are objective considerations that outweigh subjective preferences. For example: A meat market can have light green and blue-green tones, with blue lighting so that the various meats will appear fresher and redder. A pastry or candy store, on the other hand, shows advantageously in light orange, pink, white, and accents of black, stimulating an appetite for sweets.

What would you use for a bridal shop? Possibly white, correct? What about a fast food restaurant? Consider the red and yellow colors that McDonald's uses. Think about why these colors were chosen.

Using color improperly in relation to contrast or theme may have negative effects in a room. This is exactly why many people are fearful of color. When a color is used incorrectly or abused, it is labeled "difficult." There is no such thing as a bad color. Use colors correctly and in relation to the contrast or theme required.

Remember this: After careful research of the project and people involved, propose a color concept and then stick with it. You are the expert, so you make the decision. Be very careful about providing options to your client. Interior design is about decision making; otherwise, you will go crazy with options.

SUBTRACTIVE COLORS OF THE PIGMENTS

THE BASIC COLOR WHEEL CONSISTS OF A 12-HUE COLOR CIRCLE. THE *PRIMARY COLORS* ARE DEFINED IN THE CENTER TRIANGLE. ON TOP IS YELLOW, TO THE RIGHT IS RED, AND TO THE LEFT IS BLUE. BY MIXING PRIMARY COLORS, WE MAKE THE *SECONDARY COLORS*.

MIXING YELLOW AND RED YIELDS ORANGE, RED AND BLUE YIELDS VIOLET, AND BLUE AND YELLOW YIELDS GREEN.

THE TERTIARY COLORS ARE THE RESULT OF MIXING A PRIMARY WITH A SECONDARY COLOR:

YELLOW + ORANGE = YELLOW-ORANGE
RED + ORANGE = RED-ORANGE
RED + VIOLET = RED-VIOLET
BLUE + VIOLET = BLUE-VIOLET
BLUE + GREEN = BLUE-GREEN
YELLOW + GREEN = YELLOW-GREEN

ALL COLOR THEORY IS BASED ON THIS WHEEL. BY UNDERSTANDING IT, YOU WILL UNDERSTAND THE SUBTRACTIVE COLORS OF PIGMENTS.

© klick 07

165

COLOR WHEEL WITH COMPLEMENTARY CONTRASTS: SUBTRACTIVE COLORS OF THE PIGMENTS

COMPLEMENTARY COLORS ARE OPPOSITE COLORS ON THE WHEEL. WHEN PUT TOGETHER, THEY ARE CALLED *COMPLEMENTARY CONTRASTS*.

© KLICK 07

167

COMPLEMENTARY COLORS ARE DIRECTLY ACROSS FROM ONE ANOTHER ON THE COLOR WHEEL. MIXING THEIR PIGMENTS CREATES THE SAME INDE-FINABLE NEUTRAL GREY-BLACK. (BY MIXING THE OPPOSITE ADDITIVE COLORS OF THE LIGHT, YOU GET WHITE.)

REMEMBER: "ALL COLORS ARE FRIENDS OF THEIR NEIGHBORS AND LOVERS OF THEIR OPPOSITES." (MARC CHAGALL)

YELLOW AND VIOLET ARE THE STRONGEST CONTRASTS, EVEN STRONGER THAN BLACK AND WHITE.

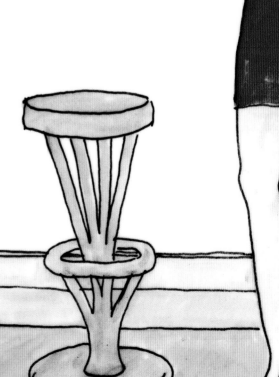

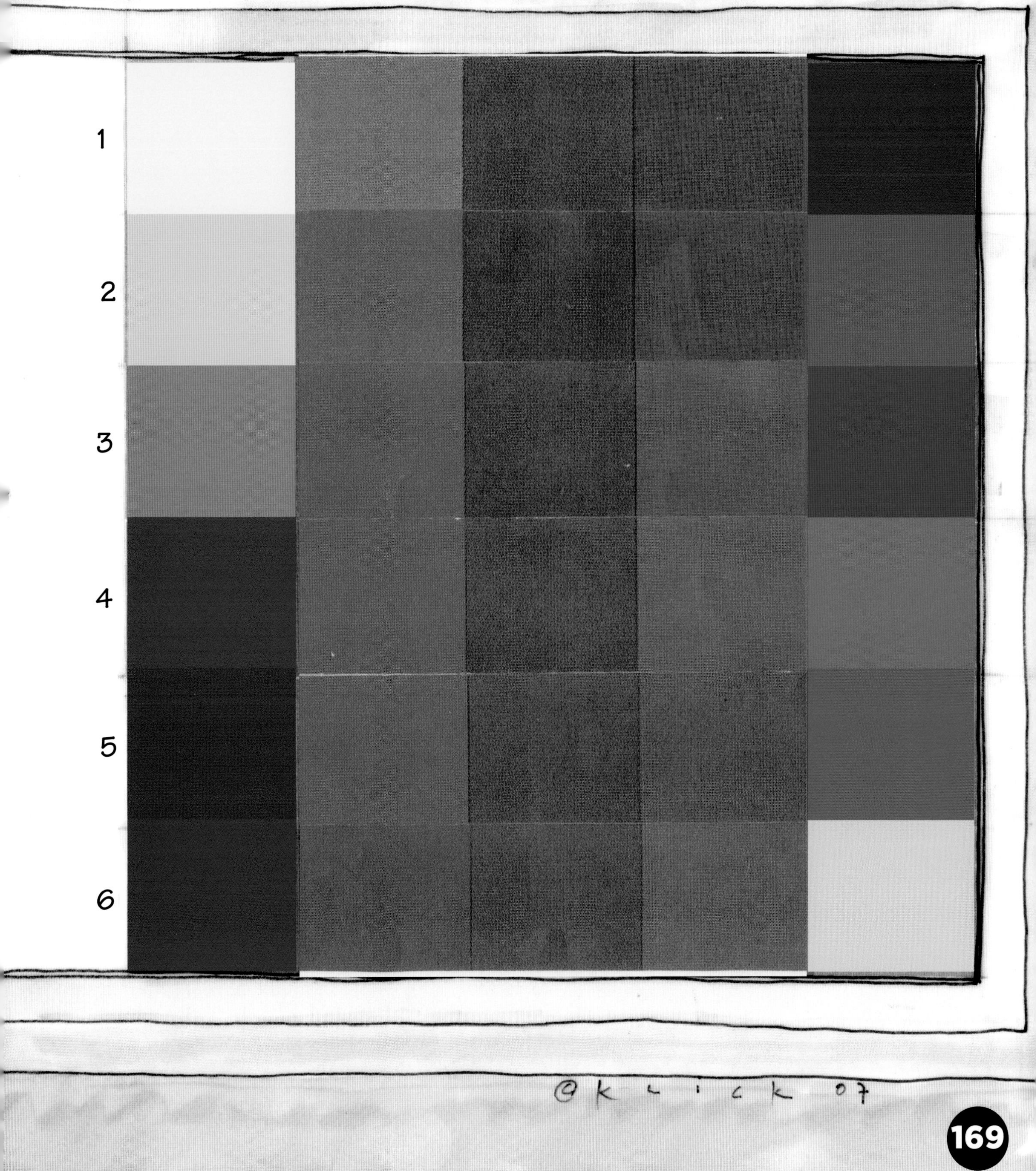

1

2

3

4

5

6

@kuick 07

SUBTRACTIVE COLORS OF THE PIGMENTS

SUBTRACTIVE COLOR REFERS TO THE PROPERTIES OF PIGMENTS, DYES, AND INKS USED IN PAINTING, COLORING, PRINTING, AND PHOTOGRAPHY. THIS TYPE OF COLOR IS WHAT IS USED IN THE DESIGN AND ART WORLDS.

THE PAINTER'S PRIMARY COLORS ARE YELLOW, BLUE, AND RED. THE PAINTER MIXES THEM WITH WHITE AND BLACK.

THE PRINTER'S PRIMARY COLORS ARE YELLOW, CYAN (BLUE), AND MAGENTA. THE PRINTER MIXES THEM WITH BLACK.

MIXING SUBTRACTIVE COLORS CAUSES THEM TO BECOME DARKER AND CLOSER TO BLACK.

© Klick 07

ADDITIVE COLORS OF THE LIGHT

ADDITIVE COLOR REFERS TO THE PROPERTIES OF LIGHT. MOST COMMONLY USED IN PHOTOGRAPHY, FILM, THEATER, AND INTERIORS.

IN THE COLORS OF LIGHT, RED, BLUE, AND GREEN ARE THE PRIMARY COLORS.

DAYLIGHT, RAINBOWS, ELECTRIC LIGHT SOURCES, CANDLES, AND FIRE ARE ALL ADDITIVE LIGHT SOURCES OR SPECTRAL COLORS.

IN MIXING ADDITIVE COLORS, THE RESULT BECOMES BRIGHTER WITH THE ADDITION OF EACH COLOR.

ADDITIVE COLOR MIXING: ADDING RED TO GREEN YIELDS YELLOW; ADDING YELLOW TO BLUE YIELDS WHITE.

LIGHTEST HUE

WARM

- SUN
- FIRE
- HEAVY
- CLOSE
- DRY

WARMEST HUE

MIXING COLORS

WE OFTEN MIX COLORS WITH EITHER WHITE OR BLACK OR WITH BLACK AND WHITE, WHICH MAKES GRAY.

PURE WHITE IS DIFFICULT TO APPLY ON LARGE SURFACES BECAUSE YOU SEE IRREGULARITIES. PAINTERS PREFER USING OFF WHITES INSTEAD. OFF WHITES ARE CREATED WHEN SMALL AMOUNTS OF OTHER COLORS ARE ADDED TO A WHITE BASE.

WHEN USING GRAY AS A BASE COLOR, BOTH WARM AND COLD GRAYS ARE USED.

YOU CAN ALSO CREATE OFF BLACKS. FOR A COOLER BLACK, ADD BLUE. FOR A WARMER BLACK, ADD RED.

WHEN MIXING COLORS, IT IS IMPORTANT THAT YOU USE THE CORRECT AMOUNT OF EACH COLOR.

THE MEANING OF COLORS

GOETHE'S COLOR WHEEL

GOETHE DESCRIBES THE CHARACTERS OF THE COLORS AS FOLLOWS: THE TEMPERATURES, EMOTIONS, PERSONALITIES, AND TRAITS.

RED

Red is a warm color.

Red is a primary color in both additive and subtractive color wheels.

Red is a very active color. When used in an interior, red can be very stimulating yet very calming through its warmth.

Red objects appear to our eye closer than they really are.

It is the second favorite color for men as well as women.

Red circles around the connotations of "blood" & "fire."

Blood: passionate (love/hate), exciting, impulsive, angry/rage (in combination with black), sexual, erotic.

Fire: heat, warmth, womb.

Red is a color full of feeling.

Red is an emotionally intense color. It enhances metabolism, respiration rate, and blood pressure.

Red colors reduce heating costs in winter.

A red car is associated with being fast.

It is a bright welcoming color. It shows enthusiasm, happiness, and interpersonal communication. Red stimulates passion, courage, and the love for life and adventure.

People identified with red usually are entrepreneurs: they are innovative and full of ideas.

Red is associated with vitality and the spirit of life and promotes decision making and self-confidence.

Red is used as an accent color to stimulate people to react, decide, and create energy.

Red can be mixed well with other red tones to create hues from orange to crimson. All the various reds work well together in a monochromatic color scheme.

BLUE

Blue is a cool color.

Blue is a primary color in both additive and subtractive color wheels.

Blue is a popular color among men and women.

Blue is associated with many positive qualities:
sympathy, harmony, friendliness, and joy.

Blue is the color of the sky and sea, which is associated with openness, the future, visionary
qualities, fantasy, and cool properties.

Blue is the color of distance, vastness, and eterni-
ty. Think of the expression "out of the blue".

It is the color of trust and dependability.

Blue is still and relaxing.

People identified with blue usually value honor,
integrity, truth, and are content.

Blue is good to balance stress, to sooth a sore
throat, and to regulate body temperature. It
slows human metabolism and produces a
calming effect.

Blue has a cooling effect. In hot temperatures,
less energy is needed to cool a blue room.

Blue is a primary healing color and encourages
peace and the ability to sleep.

When you are having trouble sleeping, try to imagine that you are wrapped in deep blue and that
it flows to each cell of your body.

In heraldry, blue is used to symbolize piety (holi-
ness) and sincerity.

If you do not know what to do, use blue.

GREEN

Green is a cool color.

Green is a primary color in the additive color wheel and a secondary color in the subtractive color wheel.

Green is the combination of blue and yellow.

Blue and yellow = green

Green is the color of nature, vegetation, and life.

Green is associated with hope, youth, rest, freshness; however, it may also associated with acerbic, sour, bitter, healthy, unripe.

Green inspires calm, security, sentimental balance, joy, positive energy, and the ability to express your feelings freely.

People identified with green usually are sensitive, kind, generous, and have a social conscience.

Green helps to neutralize bad tempers, and claustrophobia can be reduced with the power of green vibrations.

Green has a healing power.

It is the most restful for the human eye and can improve vision.

Green is the easiest color for our eyes to adapt to, especially compared to red, which requires the most time getting used to. It's "easy on the eyes." Therefore, green is used in hospitals and operating rooms for surgery.

YELLOW

Yellow is a warm color.

Yellow is a secondary color in the additive color wheel and a primary color in the subtractive color wheel.

Yellow is the color of light and sunshine. It shines everywhere and above everything. It is identified with fortune, luck, adolescence, laughter, and pleasure.

Yellow is warmth (but weaker than red).

It is associated with blooming and harvest; however, it may also be viewed as cunning and dangerous, warning, pompous, distant, painful.

It evokes pleasant, cheerful feelings.

Yellow is the color of birth, vitality, and joy.

People identified with yellow are usually full of spiritual awareness, self-confidence, and are fast learners.

This color helps to reduce negativity and anxiety.

Yellow "heats up" and excites.

Yellow may be associated with value and beauty (for example, gold or golden hair in a fairy tale).

Yellow may be both sour and refreshing (for example, lemons).

Yellow is also the color of bile when you become ill; hepatitis or "gelbsucht" in german translates as the "yellow disease."

Yellow and black are used in symbology and signage to denote toxicity and explosiveness.

Yellow and black stripes can be used for borderlines.

Note: Some yellow tones provoke excitement in a space; yet, the wrong yellow can provoke fear and suppression.

WHITE

Pure white (as compared to off-white) is a cold color.

White is the total reflection of light.

White is achieved when you mix equal parts of the three primaries of light or additive color: red, green, and blue. White is the sum of all the colors of light.

If you mix pure whites with a hint of warm color, you get a warm off-white. If you mix pure whites with a touch of a cold hue such as blue, green, or pure black colors, you get a cool off-white.

In interior design cool and warm off-whites are used often because of a lack of courage to use strong colors.

To get a gray color, you add black to a cool, off-white. By adding white to black or black to white, you will get a cool off-white or a cool off-black.

White is associated with perfection, pure, ideal, neutral, good, whole, clean, sterile, hygienic, and orderly.

Many holy figures and gurus wear the color white.

A white tablecloth makes a dining table festive.

White enables. White opens and broadens everything.

A white flag symbolizes peace.

White protects against the sun, due to its reflective qualities.

It is ultimate, godliness, angelic.

White expresses the idea of innocence, childhood, stability, and calm.

Dress in white and reload the color in your body.

White is the color of truth. White or black. Yes or no.

When you enter a white room with a black ceiling, you will tuck your head in because of its visual effect.

BLACK

Black is a cool color.

Black is the absence of light and the addition of all pigments. When the three subtractive primaries are combined, all light is absorbed and the result is a dark area of no perceptible hue.

Black is elegant.

It symbolizes seriousness, convention, and dignity.

Black is the favorite color of designers.

Black denotes strength and authority. It is considered to be very formal and prestigious (for example, black-tie event).

Black is the color of the unknown.

Black sometimes means bad luck (for example, black fridays, blackmail, blacklist).

Black is the color of the pirate flag and of other secret underground organizations.

Black hole, abyss, outer space.

Black is the color of grief, mourning, and death.

Black clothing makes us appear slender or thinner.

Black gives the feeling of perspective and depth, but a black background diminishes readability.

If you paint parts of a room in black, you create contrast and your room appears smaller.

A room painted completely in black (walls, ceiling and floor) loses all shadows and, therefore, appears larger. The room lines disappear and it feels spacey.

Black appears elegant when it is done perfectly. Otherwise, it can appear dirty due to the contrast from dust and dirt. Dust and dirt is beige or gray.

Black furniture appears to dominate a room, such as a black piano. A black closet piece appears robust (sturdier, tougher) compared to a white closet piece.

Black swallows light, but it is a great contrast to any color next to it. A black or gray background in a gallery of art or photographs makes the other colors stand out. Black contrasts well with bright colors.

As with white, we can use off-blacks. Other colors can soften black, especially blue. Black (painted walls, for example) can become a very dark blue. If you add red to black, anthracite is the result.

BROWN

Brown is a warm color.

Brown is a neutral color that can stimulate the appetite. It is found extensively in nature in both living and nonliving materials.

It is a mixture of red, blue, and yellow and has many shades and tones, each producing a different effect.

When you add white to brown, you get beige.

Brown can be a stabilizing color.

The red in brown gives it practical energy, while the yellow and blue add mental focus.

Brown gives a feeling of solidity and allows one to stay in the background, unnoticed.

Brown symbolizes earth, order, and convention.

Brown is a natural, down-to-earth color. It is found in soil, wood, and stone.

Brown represents wholesomeness. While it might be considered a little on the dull side, it also represents steadfastness, simplicity, friendliness, dependability, and health.

Brown works well as flooring because it is grounding and cozy.

Brown metal is copper or bronze.

BEIGE

Beige is a warm color.

Beige is a brown tinted with a lot of white.

Beige is used because it is very compatible with blue, red, and yellow; they are neighbors and opposites, so they relate well.

Beige with sky blue is a very good combination. It has a Mediterranean feel and is used in Greece.

Beige represents sand, and blue represents the sky.

Beige has no black in it; as soon as you add black, you end up with gray.

GRAY

There are warm grays and cool grays.

Gray is an achromatic color of any value between the extremes of black and white.

Cool grays are white mixed with black or blue.

Warm grays are white mixed with warm colors such as red and yellow.

Gray is a neutral color.

Concrete is gray.

Gray can be dull or dark: a gray, rainy afternoon.

It can mean lacking in cheer, gloomy—a gray mood.

Gray is not harsh on the eyes and neutralizes.

Gray needs an accent color or it is boring.

Gray is fog, smoke, dust, ash, dirt, and silver.

Gray can be elegant.

Gray is a balanced color.

It is a conservative color that seldom evokes strong emotion, although it can be seen as a cloudy or moody color.

Gray matter: brains, intellect.

Gray power: having to do with the elderly or senior citizens.

Like black, gray is used as a color of mourning as well as a color of formality. Along with blue suits, gray suits are part of the uniform of the corporate world. Dark, charcoal gray carries with it some of the strength and mystery of black. It is a sophisticated color without the negative attributes of black.

"Colors are rays of energy that act upon us in positive or negative ways, whether we are aware of them or not."

~ Johannes Itten

"Bunt is meine Lieblingsfarbe" (Colored is my favorite color)

~ Walter Gropius

"What use are colors to me, when I do not know how to paint?"

~ Michel Eyquem de Montaigne, Die Essais

"Color is the place where our brain and space meet."

~ Paul Cezanne

"Thoughts that come to us during the day return to us at night in color."

~ Unknown

"The world is gray, and gray is not a color."

~ Erich Kaestner

"In the weaving loom of life, every smile is a bright color; whereas every tear is a dark thread woven into the pattern. How less bright the colors would appear, if the dark colors were not there to contrast them.

~ Unknown

COLOR IN CULTURE

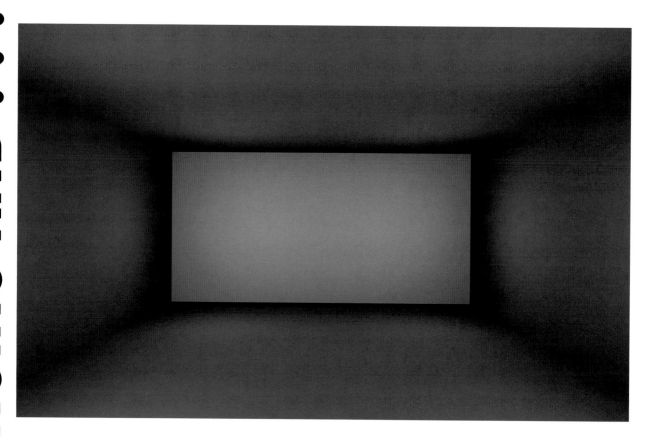

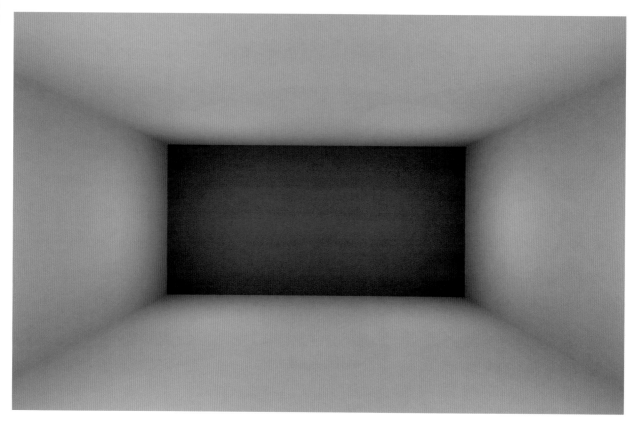

ADVANCING AND

COLORS COOL IN TEMPERATURE, LOW IN INTENSITY, AND/OR LIGHT IN VALUE APPEAR TO RECEDE.

RECEDING COLORS

COLORS OF WARM TEMPERATURE, HIGH INTENSITY, AND DARK VALUE APPEAR TO ADVANCE SPATIALLY.

THE YELLOW HOUSE

We were just married and had two sons, two years and one year old, when we bought our first house. It was a beautiful concrete house outside of Zurich, built among the green hills with a great view of the Alps on clear days.

With my newly acquired interior design skills and education, it was exciting for me to let loose and remodel our private home. The existing design had a dark brown wood-panel ceiling, white walls, rather ugly tile flooring, and a beige carpet that had to be replaced.

It was time for a new concept.

Yellow was always one of my favorite colors and is also one of the three primary colors. Yellow is sunshine, happiness, joy, excitement, and hope. This was how we felt at that time in our lives and, therefore, the decision for our color concept had to be yellow.

From the second floor to the basement, we painted the ceilings and walls in a sunny light yellow. On the floor we mounted a warm brown, industrial, hard rubber with strong, glittery quartz sand that contrasted beautifully with the sunny yellow. Standing with both feet on an earthy warm brown floor that was darker than the walls and ceiling gave you a great feeling.

We lived very happily in the yellow house for about seven years. Then Aunt Beatrice passed away and everything changed.

THE RED HOUSE

Aunt Bea was my mother's youngest sister. She lived with Uncle Hans for several years in France, and they collected antiques. Most of their antique French furniture was made out of a beautiful red-mahogany wood. When I visited my aunt and uncle's house in my younger years, I always tried to imagine what environment I would create around those old furniture pieces if and when I had the chance. Now I had inherited the furniture, and my imagination had become reality.

At this time, I was already experimenting with the color red in interior spaces. My office comprised entirely orange furniture with dark-gray-painted concrete surroundings.

But what impact would the color red have on

our lives if we were to live in a predominantly red environment? Is red an aggressive color? Red is the color of love and war. Would there be more loving or more fighting in our family? Or would there be more of both? Red is the hottest of all the warm colors.

I was anxious to find the answer to all these questions. So the concept for our remodeling became red.

I explained the concept to my wife and asked her if she would agree to this experiment of living entirely in red. She was always supporting me and answered "sure." I also asked the kids for their opinion and "mega cool" was their answer.

So we painted the ceilings, walls, doors, and window frames in fire red. We covered the

floors with various red epoxy resins poured directly from their cans. Red is an easy color to design with; all reds work together even when you add blue. From pink to purple, everything is possible. When you paint rooms in darker colors, the spaces feel larger because the contrast of the shadows is weaker and you lose your orientation more easily.

For orientation and stability in the largest living area, we painted large horizontal stripes on the walls in a darker shade of red. In the center of the house we enforced the stripes with little signal lights (LED lights).

The result was breathtaking and exciting! When arranging the furniture, we found that

colors other than red, such as blue or green, that were in the same color value matched easily. Red brought to life our inherited drab antique furniture, which took on a new personality in this environment.

Red is a great color to live with. It is complex in that it is very stimulating, inspiring, and motivating, yet at the same time surprisingly comforting and warm, like a cave or womb. The red was successful in all the rooms—the kitchen, bathrooms, living/dining room, and sleeping quarters. Red is a wonderful color for all four seasons: dark and cool in the summer and warm in the winter. During the cold months we actually used less energy for heating because we felt warmer in our red rooms!

We lived happily in the red house for about six years until we decided to sell it and move to the United States. There was only one primary color left: blue.

THE BLUE HOUSE

It was May and we had to move fast to the United States in time for our sons to begin high school. After a one-week search, we found our perfect new home: a blue ranch house from the fifties, surrounded by a forest, ponds, creeks, and oak trees. Of course, it needed major renovations.

Blue: cool and calming, the color of the sky and water. We brought all of our brown, wooden antique furniture, which gave a beautiful complementary contrast to the blue. Finding the

right blue was rather challenging. Blue is difficult when you have to match it with other colors. We painted the ceilings and walls in a blue
with a red undertone to match the furniture.
In turn, we stained the red-oak wood floors
with blue.

In the center of the house we installed a
slick blue laminate kitchen counter, added
stainless steel appliances and left it entirely
open to the dining room. We assembled the
bar on oak-tree-trunks harvested in our own
backyard and mounted it between the kitchen
and the dining area. Large mirrors were incor-
porated to make the kitchen appear double its
size and enable glimpses of the deer in our
garden when we were cooking and preparing
dishes.

We love our blue house, but when we ask ourselves which color was emotionally the best,
it's unanimous: the red house is the clear win-
ner, the yellow house comes in second, and in
third place is the blue house.

Each color has had a purpose in reflecting
our personalities and emotions and in shaping
us at the various times in our lives.

THE CONTRASTS IN ROOMS
White ceiling
Dark walls
Dark floor
Dark furniture

In this scenario your ceiling flies away. It's gone and now it's raining and snowing in your room. No coziness or sheltered feelings are possible. This is one of the most common mistakes in interior design, and you see it everywhere. It's a killer that destroys every color concept.
I hear it expressed all the time:

"We do not paint ceilings because they have to be white."

"They are always white."

"The room will look smaller when I paint the ceiling with a color other than white because darker colors make rooms look smaller."

"Yes, I would like to use colors, but not on the ceiling. I am scared to paint the ceiling. What happens if I don't like it? I'll have to repaint it white, and that is impossible."

"Ceilings have to be white because sunlight comes from above."

All of these statements are wrong. The solution to this problem lies in your color concept. If you paint your ceiling white and your walls and floor dark, you create a stark contrast between the ceiling and the rest of the room. The ceiling stands out, causing the rest of your room to appear smaller. If you eliminate this discrepancy by painting the ceiling the same color as the walls and floors, then your room feels larger than it actually is.
Less contrast = more room.

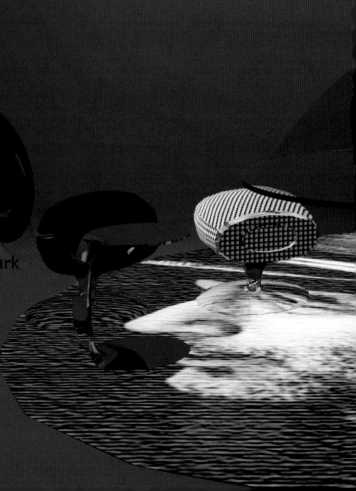

THE CONTRASTS IN ROOMS
Bright or white ceiling
Bright or white walls
Dark floor
Dark furniture

A floor that is darker than the rest of the room will always work. It has a very strong presence and reinforces the feeling of gravity. The dark furniture enhances this effect by avoiding conflict with the floor.
On our planet the color of the earth is usually darker than the sky, except when there is snow on the ground. Soil is brown, asphalt is black, grass is green, rocks are gray, and so on. In this concept the room opens up your environment and a successful pairing is created between the floor and walls.

Remember: Less contrast gives the space a larger feeling.

THE CONTRASTS IN ROOMS
Dark ceiling
White walls
White floor
Dark furniture

This scenario is scary. Your dark ceiling feels heavy, as if it is about to fall on you at any moment. It gets worse: Your dark furniture also feels cumbersome and appears as if it is falling into the abyss through the opening in your nonexistent floor.

THE CONTRASTS IN ROOMS
White ceiling
White walls
White floor
Dark furniture

The only disparity in this arrangement lies in the furniture. The white surfaces open up your room, but the dark furniture is too stark in contrast. To solve this problem, integrate the furniture with the rest of the room by repeating the white color partially in the furniture and accessories. This concept can be very playful with different patterns and surfaces.

THE CONTRASTS IN ROOMS
White ceiling
Dark walls
White floor
Dark furniture

The ceiling is open above, the floor is open below, and the dark furniture feels heavy again. However, the white ceiling balances the white floor and the dark walls have some companions in the dark furniture. In this case we are dealing with two couples, and this can be fun!

THE CONTRASTS IN ROOMS
Dark ceiling
Dark walls
Dark floor
Dark furniture

This is a great concept that shows complete harmony. There was a famous German architect whose principle concept was "less is more." The same idea applies here: Less contrast is more room. Dark rooms feel larger because they have little discord and the shadows aren't prominent. As a result, the room lines disappear and become unrecognizable. The feeling is like being in outer space without gravity. Many great opportunities are possible with this concept. You can play with subtle color changes as well as surface variations for interesting results without creating more contrast.

However, when you are using this many dark colors, beware: The darker the colors, the more maintenance you need. The color of dirt and dust is mostly beige or light gray and it stands out on dark colors. As a result, black is harder to clean than white. That's why bathroom appliances tend to be white.

THE CONTRASTS IN ROOMS
White ceiling
White walls
White floor
White furniture

This version is similar to the all-dark model. A white room does not feel quite as large as a dark room because the shadows are more pronounced. This room feels very light, youthful, heavenly, and clean. An all-white room is easy to maintain because there is little variance between the color of dirt and white surfaces. You can have much success playing with patterns, textures, and accent colors in white rooms. Don't forget, though: White can be cold.

THE CONTRASTS IN ROOMS
Dark ceiling
White walls
Dark floor
Dark furniture

This can be downright frightening and totally oppressive. Your ceiling is crushing down on you and your floor is pushing up. You are in a trash compactor! Aaaaahh! In between is the helpless furniture. You are trapped, and bad dreams are guaranteed if you use this concept in your bedroom.

This design is similar to having dark walls with a white ceiling and floor. In this case, however, the light walls connect the dark ceiling with the dark floor, but the dark furniture is not keeping the light walls company.

I do not recommend this arrangement. It is very difficult to accomplish successfully.

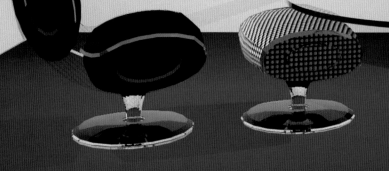

216

THE CONTRASTS IN ROOMS
Dark ceiling
White walls
Dark floor
White furniture

This combination is like the earlier example of a white ceiling, darker walls, white floor, and dark furniture but in reverse. The dark ceiling and the dark floor still create a suppressed feeling—but it can be balanced with the white furniture and walls. Try working some dark tones into the furniture via textures, patterns, and surfaces to further weave the design together. These possibilities can be very interesting.

WINDOWS

A window is an opening to the outside world. When you are designing windows, the question comes up: To what extent do you let the outside world participate in the interior environment? Furthermore, what kind of outside world are you dealing with? A suburban neighborhood or high-rise view? Factory walls or an ocean view?

At nighttime, windows on bright or white walls become black holes. In these cases window treatments (shades and blinds) are needed to reduce the clash between the walls and night view, and also to guard against inquisitive glances from people outside.

The color of windows along with their frames and treatments usually belong to the walls. When designing these elements, *use similar colors*. Work the wall colors into the textures, surfaces, and patterns of the window treatments. Only when you have a beautiful night view may you frame your window with a contrasting color.

BASEBOARDS

Like doors, windows, and their treatments, base-boards always belong to the walls and never to the floor. You see this mistake often. Sometimes the decision to do a dark baseboard on a bright wall is made because of maintenance concerns: "The dark baseboard does not show any marks or stripes from the vacuum cleaner." Wrong. This is the vacuum cleaner's problem; solve it there.

DOORS

Doors and their frames typically belong to the walls, so stay away from contradictory colors when composing these elements. If your door is special and you want to make a bold statement, then creating a contrast is an effective way to show it off. In ancient times, farmers used the blood of an ox to paint their entry door red. Over the ages the use of ox blood disappeared, but red entry doors can still be seen today in suburban homes.

DOORS, BASEBOARDS, AND WALLS

Is your door a beautiful one? If not, your door should remain silent and unnoticed. Do not distract your company with an ugly door. The only time you should make your door stand out is when your design concept calls for it.

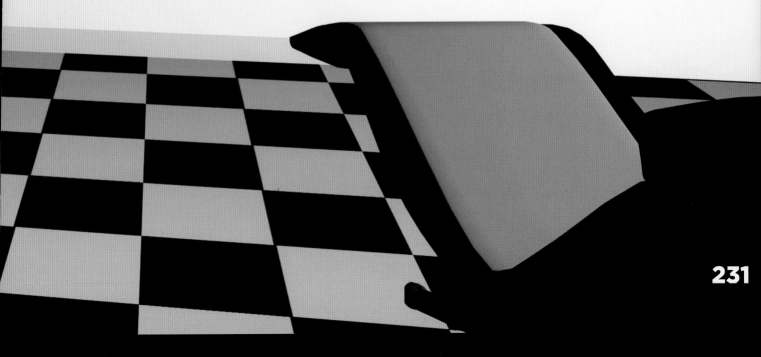

TRIM, MOLDINGS, PANELING, AND WAINSCOTING

There is no balance in this room because the contrast is too strong. This is not a good solution unless your concept calls for this type of contrasting theme. If it does, then make the contrasts stronger and the moldings larger to make it successful.

The balance is better, but the room is still ugly.

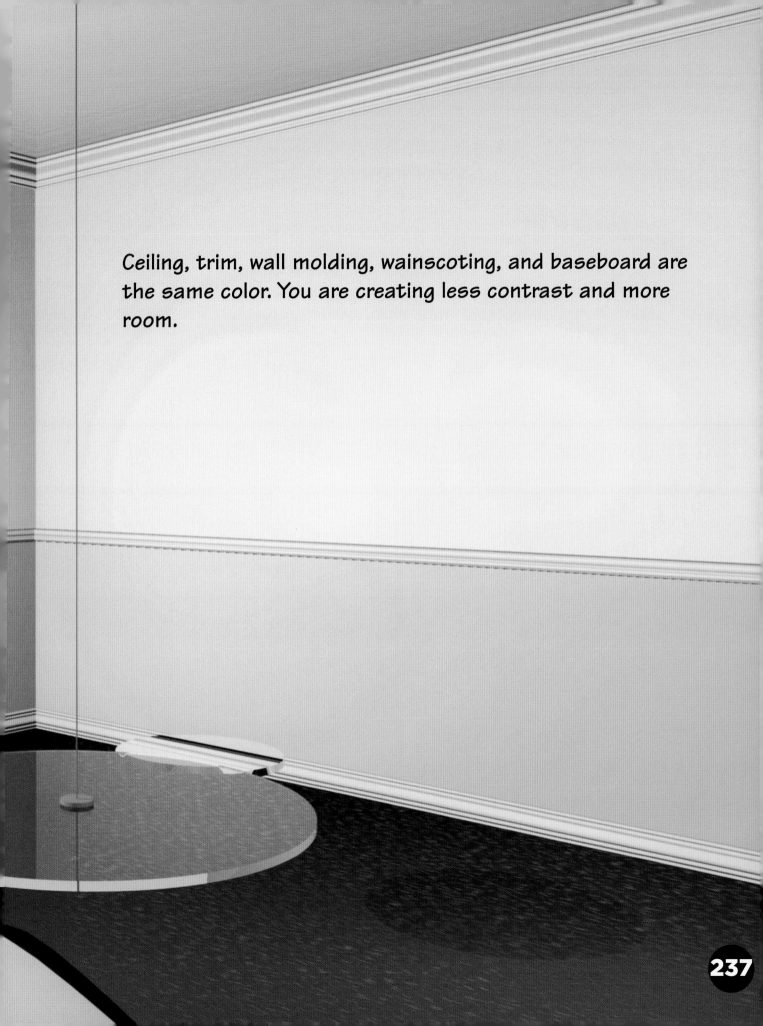

Ceiling, trim, wall molding, wainscoting, and baseboard are the same color. You are creating less contrast and more room.

RESIDENTIAL INTERIOR DESIGN: WHERE WE STAND

We all know them. We see them almost every day in color and on high-gloss papers; in brochures, flyers, inserts, and advertising; in newspapers, in magazines, on TV shows; and in commercials: Residential interiors created by realtors, developers, and marketing and sales people from furniture stores. Decorators with zero skills. Faulty and mis-arranged design made in indescribable ugliness. Design without concept, knowledge, or style — just a bunch of incongruous "new stuff." A motley crowd of materials, colors, furniture, objects, and lights piled up in a room. Larger, bigger, newer . . . and if we ask the designers why they are doing this, the answer is, "that's what our clients ask for, that's what everyone likes, and that's what we sell the best."

It is we, the consumers, who are to blame. It is our lifestyle and taste that matters and will make the difference. So, we begin with ourselves. We are missing the icons we once had. Where is the Jackie O. of this century? Where are the Eames and Mies of today? In the 1950s, 1960s, and 1970s, the United States defined lifestyles and exported these designs to Europe and around the world. The indestructible is not exportable. Let us think larger and more globally.

HOME SWEET HOME, WHAT DO WE DO WITH YOU?

Here is a new tool for you to use: The Residential Interior Designer's Survival Kit.

The top five actions needed for The Residential Interior Designer's Survival Kit are as follows:

1. Discover yourself
2. Create a concept
3. Be consistent
4. Utilize the contrasts: color, light, and shadow
5. Learn to arrange

1. Discover yourself. Research yourself. It's about your personality. What do you like? What style? *Breakfast at Tiffany's* or *West Side Story?* What fashion? Dolce & Gabbana or Martha Stewart? Where do you shop? Wal-Mart or Target? What art do you like? Kinkade or Koons? What colors? Black or beige? Orange or blue? Yellow or violet? Blue and brown? White? Light blue and beige? What time period? The past from Colonial times? Today's contemporary? Tomorrow's futuristic? What music? Opera or rock 'n' roll? Mozart or Pearl Jam? What architecture? Frank Gehry or Prince Charles? What material? Wood or plastic? Nylon or cotton? Natural or technical? What forms? Organic or angles? What country? France or Japan? What landscape? Rocky Mountains or Virgin Islands? Mediterranean or desert? What cultures? Native American or African? What food? Cheeseburger or chateaubriand?

Open your eyes to the world you are living in and educate yourself. Go to your library or online and do some research; read lifestyle, fashion, and living magazines. Be careful when watching interior design shows on television; many mistakes are evident. Learn from the experts.

When doing an interior design job for someone else or a

client, use his or her personality instead of yours in answering the above questions.

2. Create a concept. Now you need a concept. It's all about the concept. Without a concept there is no good design. Within the overall concept you also need a color, material, and light concept. Finding the right concept can be difficult. Use the knowledge about yourself or your client to create it. For example:

You like beige, yellow, Martha Stewart, and Old World.
That could be a beige room with homey furniture arranged with daisy and Colonial furniture.

You like black, Dolce & Gabbana, and Japan.
That could be black furniture in a white room with bamboo flooring.

You like blue, Mozart and contemporary.
That could be a blue room with a rococo chandelier and an Eames lounge chair.

You like Native America, orange, and Pearl Jam.
That could be a red room with white dashes and orange furniture.

You like Old World, blue, and brown.
That could be a blue room with antique wooden furniture.

3. Be consistent. You have to decide what concept you would like to use. Then start doing research in the field of your chosen concept. The library is always a great source, as well as the Internet, bookstores, and travel catalogues. Collect and copy samples: color (paint) samples, fabric samples, floor samples, wood samples, furniture catalogues, and light catalogues. Go shopping. Make a plan and a budget. Prepare your color concept, material concept, and light concept.

4. Utilize the contrasts of color, light, and shadow. Color is part of our lives, so use it—but beware! You are using color in three dimensions and you are dealing with space: floors, walls, and ceilings. Generally, we can say the floor should be darker than the walls and the ceiling. If you are using darker colors on the floor and walls, then you have to include the ceiling, too. If you don't do so, your ceiling will "fly away." This is one of the most common mistakes in interior design.

Be aware of the contrasts. They are essential to your concept. Contrasts can be good or bad. They can work for or against your concept. Using one similar tone and different materials with various finishes is an easy way to achieve success. In doing so, you can avoid bad contrasts.

Generally, the more colors you use, the more difficult it becomes to maintain a sense of unity. If you use more than one or two colors, you have to repeat them. Colors that stand in contrast do not like to be alone. Being alone is boring. They need relatives and friends. They need to communicate. The same thing goes for when you dress yourself. Earrings should match your necklace. Black shoes, black belt, and black handbag.

Darker colors can make your room feel larger. It's true. With darker colors, you lose the shadows and the wall lines disappear. In a black or dark-colored room your orientation is lost. You cannot recognize where the walls end and the ceiling begins. The difference between where the floor meets the walls becomes unrecognizable. It feels like you're in space. Bright colors are a great contrast in a black or dark room. Of course, you have to illuminate a dark room with stronger and brighter lights. A lot of light is lost in dark rooms, but the effect on the color contrast is great.

Walls have windows. The window is part of the wall. At night when it is dark outside your window is a black hole in the wall, especially when your wall is painted a light color such as white or beige. It creates an extremely strong contrast. That is why window treatments are used. Your wall and window treatment should be similar in tone. They belong together.

5. Learn to arrange. Arranging usually comes at the end of each project and it is a lot of fun. Be sure your dimensions are correct and the furniture fits. Of course, you started with all the dimensions earlier. If you would like to sketch a plan; use a larger scale; 1/4 inch or 1/2 inch is easier. Be careful with scaled templates; they invite you to make mistakes. Dimensions don't forgive when you make mistakes. If you do not know how to sketch a plan in scale, you can always mark the sizes on the floor with tape. Everyone did this a few hundred years ago. Chalk and sawdust were used in ancient times.

Group objects and create islands; do not let the pieces fly around. You need a reason for something to stand alone. It has to be part of your concept.

When hanging pictures, the average eye level should be about 5 feet, 6 inches. A picture should be mounted one-third of its height above 5 feet, 6 inches, no higher. Large size pictures start about 1 foot from the floor.

Above all, have fun with your project! Interior design is exciting!

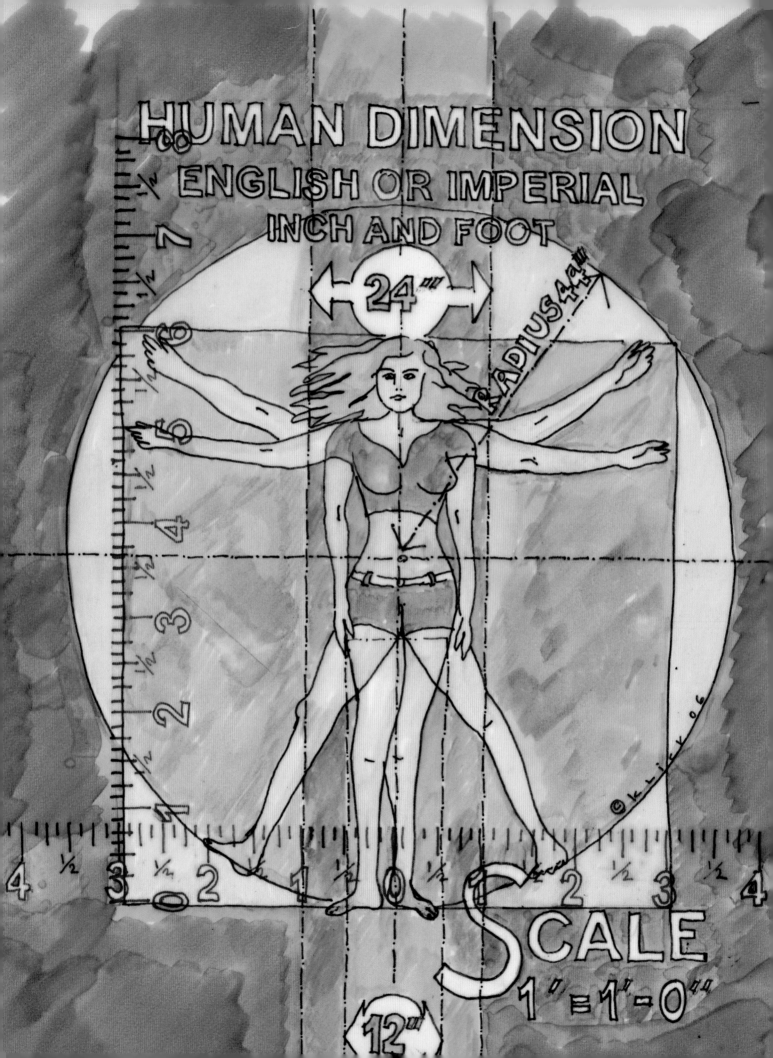

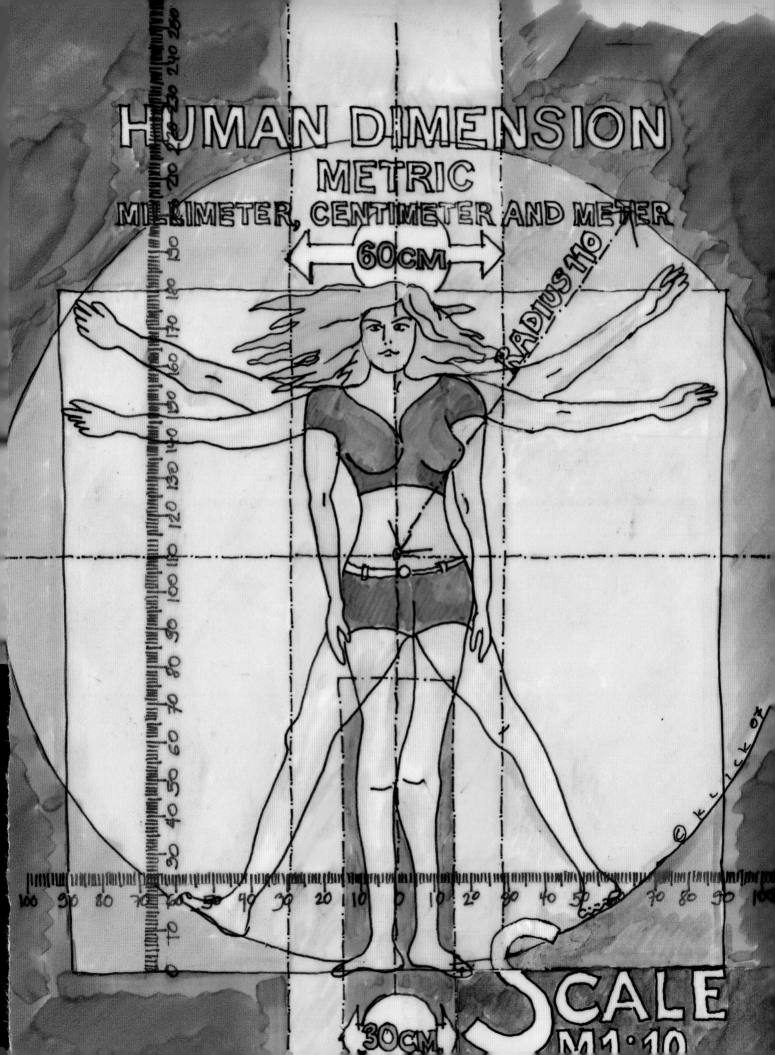